Dimensions & the Awakening of the Divine Consciousness

Understanding Earth's Journey from 3rd to 5th Dimension

Dr. Heather Anne Harder

LIGHT PUBLISHING

Crown Point, IN 46307

Limits of Liability, warning, and Disclaimer
This book is written for informational, educational and entertainment purposes. The authors/ publisher of this book and accompanying materials have used best efforts in preparing this program and make no representation or warranties with respect to the accuracy, applicability, fitness, or completeness of the contents of this program. They shall not be liable for any misuse of this material nor guarantee that anyone following these suggestions, techniques, tips, ideas, or strategies will experience the same results, and shall have neither liability nor responsibility to anyone with respect to any results either directly or indirectly by the information contained. The author and publisher disclaim any warranties (expressed or implied), merchantability, or fitness for any particular purpose. The authors and publisher shall in no event be held liable for any loss or other damages including, but not limited to, special, incidental, consequential, or other damages. The authors and publisher don't warrant the performance, effectiveness or applicability of any sites listed in this book. All links are for information purposes and are not warranted for content, accuracy or any other implied or explicit purposes. This book contains the opinions and ideas of its author. It is intended to provide helpful and informative material on the subject it covers. It is not intended to act as a substitute for professional services as needed. If the reader requires personal or professional assistance or advice, a competent professional should be consulted.

Published by

LIGHT PUBLISHING

1611 W 94th Place, Crown Point, IN 46307
219-662-7248
www.lightpublishing.net   www.HeatherHarder.com
Email: Heather@HeatherHarder.com
ISBN 978-1-884410-15-4
Printed in the United States of America
Light Publishing books are available at special quantity discounts for bulk purchases. Special books, or book excerpts, can be created to fit your specific needs. Call for details.

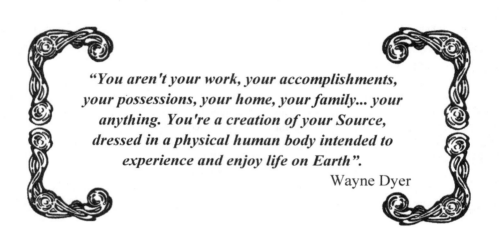

"You aren't your work, your accomplishments, your possessions, your home, your family... your anything. You're a creation of your Source, dressed in a physical human body intended to experience and enjoy life on Earth".

Wayne Dyer

FREE BONUS: Access your Divine Meditation Experience

There are some things that just can't be written. Explaining a Multidimensional Journey is one such thing. Therefore if you go to www.heatherharder.com/dimensionresources you can access the meditation designed to take you through a virtual journey through the dimensions. This meditation will help you learn to recognize and feel the physical shifts in your body as you move through the various vibrational densities. It will help you experience, recognize, and take mastery over the shifting dimensions in your life. This is how you will learn to connect with Source and your multidimensional consciousness.

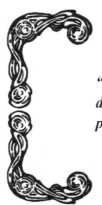

"You have to change your thinking if you desire to have a future different from your present."

Germany Kent

DEDICATION/ACKNOWLEDGMENT

It is with great pleasure that I dedicate this book to each and every person who has touched my heart and life. This journey through the dimensions is a journey of soul awakening. It is a sacred honor to be on this journey with you. Indeed your questions and comments have helped mold me and my writings. Now it is time to lovingly release this book back to you, my beloved reader, and trust that its contents will touch your heart, awaken your soul, and activate your cellular memory. It is the truth that will set you free. ***Dimensions & the Awakening of Divine Consciousness*** represents my basic human understanding of an extremely complex system and years of learning condensed down to this single simple volume. ***Dimensions & the Awakening of Divine Consciousness*** is meant to help illustrate the vast journey that this planet and its people are on. It tells of our voyage and what awaits us. Together we must walk through the illusion of life and recognize the truth that life on Earth is a game designed for our pleasure and growth and it is changing. Together we can move into a 5th-Dimensional understanding and higher awareness. We must awaken into the divine realization that we are spiritual masters who have come to Earth to express our divinity in a physical world. And in doing so, we are collectively creating a massive transformation that will impact every aspect of our life. ***Dimensions & the Awakening of Divine Consciousness: Understanding Earth's Journey from 3rd to 5th Dimension*** is given to you as a gift from my heart to yours.

My deep and sincere appreciation goes to all those who contributed to the success of this book. You are blessed and have deeply blessed me.

The key to growth is the introduction of higher dimensions of consciousness into our awareness.

Lao Tzu
Ancient Chinese philosopher and writer
6th century B

Preface

Preparing to be Stretched

I am a teacher. I've always been a teacher. It is what I do. When I was six I built my first school in my backyard with my dad's scrap lumber. It had a roof, and a floor, and four walls, and I would gather the neighborhood kids together and keep them for the day teaching the lessons. Over the years my classroom has changed, my content has changed, but I know how important my content is to a changing world. I trust you will find this content relevant.

When my daughter learned about my new writing project, she wanted to protect me. She lovingly said, "Most people aren't going to understand that. You can't use that kind of title because it's going to scare people off."

She is probably right. What is normal for me and you, can be scary for others. New information can jerk us out of our comfort zone and pitch us into the dark unknown. I remember being startled by some of the things that were shared with me by my spirit friends. It would bring up anxiety when I would be told strange new things. It would take me a while to process it so that I could share it with my readers and make it fit into my world.

Much of what I'm going to share with you may strike you the same way. Just embrace it, bless it, ask to know truth, and just move on. You don't have to accept it, nor should you reject it. Better to set it aside and let it simmer. Truth will always present itself.

Ever since the group The 5th Dimension sang the song, "This is the dawning of the age of Aquarius," we're been hearing about this fifth dimension and humanity's movement from one dimension to another. For some of this, it makes sense, for some of it doesn't, and the vast majority didn't care or think about it.

But hearing about humanity's movement from 3rd to 5th dimension brings about a lot of questions for me. What does that mean? How will it affect me? What is my role?

And that is what we're going to talk about in this book, ***Dimensions & the Awakening of Divine Consciousness: Understanding Earth's Journey from 3rd to 5th Dimension***.

When I am given information about the dimensions, I am not given words or even facts. I am given experiences. In this case, I was taken on a journey. It was during the day. I was wide awake. I was told to relax on the couch. I was guided to get rid of all disruptions so that nothing with interrupt our excursion. Then I was taken on the journey through the dimensions so that I could have my own virtual tour in consciousness. My body never moved, yet I experienced the reactions, the feelings, the thoughts, the changes in my mind and body as I went through these dimensions. (I will talk about this again later on.)

I am going to do my best to describe what I experienced and learned. There was never a voice that explained things. I was aware of a companion but very saw or heard anything or anyone else. In the end, I am left to explain my experiences in our limited physical-based language. I am forced to use the words, concepts, and language structure that I know to explains things that do not fit our experience or language.

It is very difficult to describe concepts and experiences in a way that makes sense to our minds. If our mind doesn't understand it, it just rejects it. As always, I strongly suggest that you affirm to know truth. You need to learn your truth and be open to truth in the process.

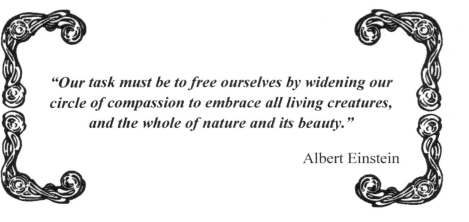

"Our task must be to free ourselves by widening our circle of compassion to embrace all living creatures, and the whole of nature and its beauty."

Albert Einstein

CONTENTS

~1~
Understanding the Relationship between Dimensions, Planet Earth, and Your Amazing Life

"String theory envisions a multiverse in which our universe is one slice of bread in a big cosmic loaf. The other slices would be displaced from ours in some extra dimension of space."

Brian Greene

Dimensions are shifting.

Human consciousness is evolving.

You were born, and someday you will die. In between is a great adventure.

Just as Sherlock Holmes set out to solve his crime mysteries using only a few clues and his powerful deductive reasoning, so too are we destined to figure out how life works and take mastery over it. Can you imagine how much more challenging it would have been for Sherlock to solve his crimes if his mind kept changing? Indeed, ours is. The mind, complete with its own consciousness, is evolving and thus the world around us is also changing. In this book, I will do my best to explain what is happening and why. Most importantly, how you can take mastery over it.

I first discovered the reality of the dimensions when I was working with a young man in his early twenties. He thought he was going crazy because his mind was out of control and kept changing. (Think ADHD on steroids.) Everything in his world was never the same from one minute to the next. Since he wasn't on any medications and wasn't taking recreational drugs, he thought he was losing his mind. As I worked with him, I discovered the problem. He wasn't anchored in his current dimension, and would randomly flip from one dimension to another. Much like a person on LSD, his world and reality would shift with each dimensional flip. As I taught him to anchor in a dimension, he overcame his challenge.

For most of us, our dimensional shifts are much more subtle and less dramatic. Our shifting is more of a fading in and out of a dimensional consciousness. Most people that I have worked with have experienced a slight shifting. Just like them, you are experiencing the dimensional drift whether you realize it or not.

The world is changing, you are changing, and what your mind perceives is changing. Do you feel like you have less control over your mind now? Are you experiencing a random range of thoughts or beliefs? Do you have thoughts that seem to come out of nowhere? Do you have moments of clarity only to get lost, once again, in a mental fog? No, it isn't your diet or product of your age or early onset dementia. More than likely, it is the product of your shifting dimensions. The more you understand it, the easier it becomes to control it.

Pretend you are a water skier being pulled behind a boat. On the skis, you have control over lots of things that can enhance or diminish your experience. Balance, some direction, and posture are under your control, but it is the boat that pulls you along. The boat also controls many aspects of your experience, like speed and duration. If you lose your balance behind the boat, you also lose all control and your skiing experience is much less pleasant.

Your ***mind consciousness*** is like the skier. It is yours alone but it is being affected by the boat, which represents the greater ***collective consciousness***. Both your individual consciousness and the collective consciousness are impacted by the ***dimensional reality*** in which you operate. Let's call this dimensional reality, the weather. The higher the dimensional reality, the more beautiful the weather. Your skiing comfort and enjoyment is greatly impacted by the dimension that you are in. Even though your skiing performance may be the same, the weather will greatly impact your experience.

Most of us are born in a good, solid third-dimensional reality. Everything that is real is defined by our five senses like sight, touch, smell, hearing, and taste. Over the last five decades, Earth is slowly shifting into higher dimensional consciousness. The planetary collective shift, like the boat, impacts the individual, like the person on the ski, and vice versa. Although one person doesn't control the collective, one person does influence it.

We are each influencing and being influenced by the collective dimensional shift. Together we are also shifting Earth's dimensions and the collective consciousness as well as being influenced by them.

Okay now, let's use another example.

Think glasses. You can put them on and you can take them off at will. Each pair of glasses are different, some are defined by colors. Some make things appear upside down, some make things look bigger, some smaller, some fuzzy, some clear. Get the idea? Each pair of glasses changes your world, yet it doesn't. It just changes how you perceive your world.

Let's say you put on the glasses with red lenses. Everything you look at is tinted red. Now everywhere you look you see red because of the impact of the glasses with the red lenses. Red now dominates your world, thus your world has changed. Yet it hasn't. Take off the red glasses, and put on a pair of glasses with green lenses. Now your world has shifted, everywhere you look you see green. You and your world have shifted, and yet it is fundamentally the same.

The glasses are like your dimensional reality. Every time you shift dimensional reality consciousness, the world that you perceive changes. You are perceiving through new lenses (i.e. dimensions). As you shift dimensions, you are seeing your world through new glasses everything has changed. The greater the number of people looking through the same glasses/dimensions, the more the collective earth consciousness shifts. As the earth consciousness/dimensions shift, your glasses change like it or not. Everything changes and yet nothing changes. The whole impacts the individual and the individual affects the whole.

Let's do another example. In the 1950's, the Earth was firmly tied to third-dimensional reality. Most of the world thought/perceived in a 3D-based way. Third-dimensional thinking is based on duality; me versus you, right versus wrong, absolutes and no shades of gray (not even fifty shades). This thinking/perceiving shaped our reality. It was defined by edges or absolutes. (You may be asking yourself "What about 4th Dimension?" Have patience, we will discuss the role of 4th Dimension later.)

Consciousness is still evolving. Let's look back and see how far we have come. In the 1880s, little Elizabeth was ten years old and was beaten so badly that the neighbors complained of the noise. She was chained to a bed, scissors pierced her cheeks, not a single person did anything to stop it or intervene. Parents could do whatever they wanted, no laws would stop them. Then along came one social worker who took action. Elizabeth finally got her day in court although she had to be carried in on a stretcher. This lone social worker had found a law that protected animals. She argued that Elizabeth, as a human animal, deserved the same protection as a dog. The laws were changed.

When Christina Crawford, adopted daughter of a beloved movie star at the time, Joan Crawford, wrote a book detailing her mother's abusive behavior, people were horrified and outraged. Her book, ***Mommie Dearest*** (1978) sent shock waves around the country. It wasn't the abuse that shocked and appalled people, it was the fact that Christina wrote the book disclosing the family's secrets (after all, secrets were a part of family life). Christina was villainized for attacking her mother. Her book escalated the national discussion on child abuse, but it would be decades before the dimensional consciousness of the planet would evolve to where Christina Crawford would be viewed compassionately, as the victim of abuse.

Now, many years later, we have collectively said, "Abuse and mistreatment of anyone at any age, will not be accepted." That is evidence of consciousness evolving. Each of us is a vital part of this evolution. No one is exempt; you may be one of the early risers like the social worker or Christina Crawford or you may be one that's carried along for a while, but everyone is on this journey. Our history books are filled with those people who have changed our world because they saw things differently. We have been truly blessed by their presence. Most of our shift leaders had to defend themselves against the masses, like Christiana or Elizabeth. Some were even martyred for their cause.

Think about your life and the world in which you live. Who thinks differently? Be open to your changing view of the world, it is impacted by and impacts the dimensions in which the earth resides. This book was designed to help you understand each dimension and the gift it brings, as well as the opportunity it presents.

Collectively and currently, the earth is on a transition course to progress from the third dimension to the fifth dimension and you, my friend, are my part of the journey.

~2~

Become a Truth Seeker

"I like to engage the public because when I was in high school, I had all these questions about anti-matter, higher dimensions and time travel. Every time I went to the library, every time I asked people these questions, I would get some strange looks. Nobody could answer any of these questions."

Michio Kaku

Life is filled with information, some helpful and some not so helpful. Some of the information is truth and some not. Learning to identify the truth, the important truth is vital to living a purposeful life. Whether you are reading or listening to my words or someone else's, it is vital that you shield yourself from anything except the truth. It is time to become a truth seeker.

A truth seeker yearns for and seeks the essence of the truth in every word and situation. Truth seekers are compelled like Dick Tracy or Sherlock Holmes, to follow clues until they are certain of the truth. If *you* are not willing to be tenacious and ferret out the truth in every situation, then you are not yet a truth seeker. The pursuit of truth must be continual; in life situations, you cannot be an occasional truth seeker.

Finding truth is not always easy. The truth is often colorfully wrapped in perceptions—think of rose-colored glasses—and biased by emotions. Some people use truth like a protective shield against adversity. But truth used cruelly can also be a painful, cutting sword. Seeking to understand truth can, like the sword, help protect you from distractions and confusion. Truth can be the fuel to move you along your life's path and bring growth. Real growth can be difficult and sometimes painful. There, it is important to seek truth mindfully and consistently.

The Bible warns, *beware of false prophets*. It foretells a time when even God's most elite will be fooled. *What?! Even God's most elite will be fooled.* Surely God's most elite will be discerning and recognize and reject falsehoods! What kind of individuals could fool God's best? These *false prophets* must be incredibly believable to be so convincing. They are either great cons or believe in what they are teaching.

False prophets, convincing arguments, and even persuasive marketing are but a few of the distractions that surround you daily. You are flooded with information in a variety of forms every minute of the day; books, newspapers, newsletters, magazines, television, radio and the internet bombard you with information. Experts in every field offer workshops and proclaim the truth of their insights. It is your duty to take the time to sort the important from the unimportant. Sift reality from illusion and identify the truth from the misinformation. Don't despair—this is easier than it sounds. To still the noise and effectively sort out the truth, you only need to "set the intention" and ask for Divine help.

Setting the intention to know truth requires no special ceremony or ritual. Remember it is not the formula or special words you use; it is the intention you set. It happens in your heart and mind instantly once you make the conscious choice to pursue truth. So right now, in your own way, make your intention to know truth and not be distracted by anything that is not truth for you. It is important to do this every day. Asking for Divine help is even easier. Just do it in prayer, affirmation or intention. Send an invitation from your heart. Even though the intention to discern truth is important and easy, we often don't think about it. For many of you, it hasn't been a priority. I offer the following "Truth Seekers Mantra" as a tool to help you recognize truth and release everything else more quickly and easily. Say it with conviction, as a prayer or affirmation, before reading, watching television, listening to the news or to other people's information in any form. Start each day by saying it. After three weeks of constant use, it will be ingrained in your mind. You will be surprised at the difference it makes.

The truth seeker's mantra:

> *I easily recognize truth and I willingly release all that is not truth. Every word I speak and thought I think is a reflection of my truth. Every day in every way my ability to discern truth and my willingness to accept truth grows. I accept truth where and how I find it—peacefully, joyfully and harmoniously integrating it into my totality. Let my path of truth take me ever closer to my greatest potential and good. I am the love, strength, courage, and perseverance required to walk my path of truth for now and evermore.*

I trust this mantra will serve you as you move through the avalanche of information that you face every day.

My intention is to give you only truth. But as I convert my experiences to words, concepts, and beliefs, I can misrepresent truth. I may distort truth. Therefore getting in the habit of being shielded from anything that is not truth is vital.

I look forward to hearing your experiences as you begin to adapt this mantra into your everyday life. I wish you great success and much love on your journey as a truth seeker.

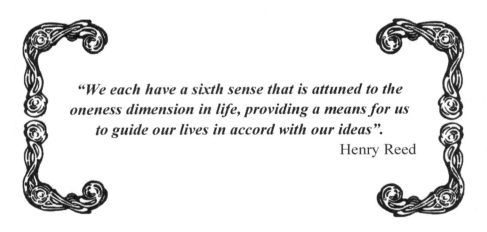

"We each have a sixth sense that is attuned to the oneness dimension in life, providing a means for us to guide our lives in accord with our ideas".
Henry Reed

~3~

How I Learned about the Dimensions

"As long as habit and routine dictate the pattern of living, new dimensions of the soul will not emerge."

Henry Van Dyke

In my book, **_Many Were Called Few Were Chosen: The Story of Mother Earth and the Earth-based Volunteers_**, I describe the journey of Mother Earth and those who have chosen to help with her transformation from a 3rd to a 5th-dimensional planet. Since then I have read many different descriptions of what that means. But that is not how I learned about the dimensions.

My understanding of the dimensions didn't come from something I read or was told. Instead while awake, during the day, I was taken on a virtual journey through the universe. I call this process a "field trip in consciousness" since my body lay quietly on the couch while I journeyed beyond the rational realm. A very *real* spirit being guided my consciousness out of my body and visually showed me how dimensions and this planet operate. I experienced it as if it was happening in my body, but it was true "an out of body" experience. No words were ever spoken although there was some conscious communication. As I journeyed through the universe, I experienced the vibratory changes. I also experienced the dimensional reality shifts and saw how they impacted the physical body. I saw and experienced everything. It was an amazing journey that forever changed me and my understanding about the life we are living.

These experiences are not easy to explain since we lack the conceptual understanding and vocabulary to properly frame them. I simply promise to do my best. After all, this is my life purpose. I am here to help humanity understand, accept, and assimilate their world and their own greatness.

As I attempt to describe the Earth's vibratory dimensional nature to you, understand that much of what I experienced is beyond my ability to describe with words and concept. This book is my humble attempt to share my wondrous journey and the lessons I learned on that day. As you read my words, affirm to know and recognize truth. Allow your head and soul to experience the vibration of my words and you will be changed by them. Let your mind relax and ask your heart to absorb the truth and only the truth.

Understanding frequency and vibrations:
In order to fully appreciate this Earth mission and the Lightworkers (Earth-based volunteers) sent to assist with this great planetary transformation, you must first understand the nature of Earth. To understand the nature of Earth, you must understand the nature of the vibratory frequency and dimensions and their role in creating reality.

The term *dimension* is used frequently on Earth, even though few fully understand its true meaning. This was intentional. On Earth, our world is defined and controlled with words. The vocabulary must often be introduced to the planet before achieving full comprehension of its meaning. Star Trek gave us a language for space exploration while the singing group, The Fifth Dimension, taught us about, "the dawning of the age of Aquarius."

Everything in the universe is alive...filled with movement and animation. Our scientists have understood atomic energy for a while now. We were taught in school, that the movement of the atomic parts (protons, neutrons, and electrons) differ with each type of atom. This movement is what I refer to as the frequency vibration. The speed and type of movement vary with each type of particle and the energy that particle carries. You have this energy frequency and it changes easily. What you eat, do, associate with, and think have a great impact on your vibration. Your vibratory frequency changes just like Chicago weather and your moods. Remember the sixties...with its good and bad vibes? These were introductory lessons.

Understanding Dimensions:
A dimension is a state of being, an orientation to all life experiences; it is a state of consciousness or mindfulness. Each dimension carries with it a vibratory frequency range. This frequency moves you in and out of a consciousness pattern. It determines your underlying consciousness reality and that in turn affects the way you perceive your life experiences. It does not affect the experience—only the way your experience is framed.

As an example; if driver A exists in a third-dimensional reality and experiences an angry driver on the road, he may feel provoked and engage in a battle to defend himself (remember the third dimension is framed with me vs. you; right vs. wrong, etc.). Driver A may feel his honor has been challenged and most likely will take it personally. But if a fifth-dimensional driver B experiences the same situation, he may smile and send love to the unhappy person. He would understand that anger is a reflection of the person experiencing the anger and not feel compelled to react or defend himself. The same experience would bring about different reactions based on the dimensional consciousness of the person experiencing it.

There are many factors that will determine whether the above driver is vibrating at a third or fifth-dimensional level. Both driver A and B could be the same person, operating at different levels at different times. It is not the experience but the consciousness that determines the quality of a person's life experience.

Using the theater as a metaphor for life on Earth, the dimension is the temperature, lighting, and air quality within the building. It is not the scenery or script. The dimension determines the comfort level, but it doesn't determine the action in the play.

If the actor is in a well-lit, well-ventilated, comfortable environment, he will greatly enjoy the drama, whether or not he is playing a poor peasant or a rich and handsome leading character and whether or not he is acting in a country setting or a city setting. The reverse is also true—if it is too hot or too cold or if the air is unpleasant—the actor will find less joy, no matter what role he played or in what setting the role happened. His misery would detract from whatever role he happens to be playing. More than likely the actor would continue with his part, but his enjoyment and comfort would be greatly affected.

As these examples illustrate, a dimensional state is neither a place nor a physical state as some people believe. You may say, "I live in the third dimension," or "I live in a third-dimensional world." In truth, dimensions are not a place or a location; rather, they are the perspective or attitude from which one views his personal life experiences. The dimension reflects the state of consciousness.

Each dimension has a frequency range—the higher the frequency, the higher the dimension. Frequency limits or expands one's perception; the higher the frequency, the more encompassing the perception. The higher the frequency (and therefore the dimensional state)the more joy and freedom found in any life circumstance. The higher the frequency, the more love and light one allows into his or her life. The higher the frequency, the more expanded the state of conscious awareness of the individual. The higher the consciousness the more expanded the mindfulness and the greater perspective one has of their world.

All frequencies and dimensional states provide an opportunity for growth. Existence in any form is about growth. Lessons are forever.

One dimension is not better or worse than another, just as kindergarten is neither better nor worse than first grade. They are just different experiences and appropriate for different periods of development. They offer unique experiences and allow different lessons. You must go through one level to be ready for the next.

Have you ever gone to a 3-D movie and been given 3-D glasses? If you watch the movie with the glasses you have one set of perceptions and if you take them off, the movie experience changes. You could watch the movie without the glasses, but when you put on the glasses and viewed the movie through those simple and inexpensive paper and plastic glasses, your movie experience changed. The movie was the same movie, but how you viewed it changed. You experienced the movie with an illusion of greater depth and realism with the glasses. So it is with dimensions. Each dimension is unique and gives its own particular experiences. As humanity moves through the dimensional awareness, they do not lose the old perspective, it is only enhanced and expanded. There is greater awareness and you are more mindful of the new reality.

Dimension reflects the state of conscious awareness and the dimension is a factor of their vibratory frequency.

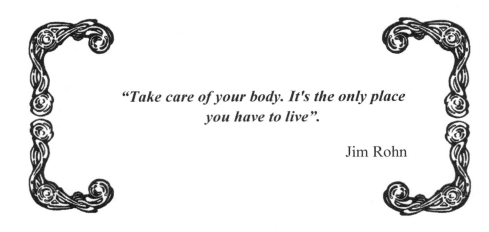

"Take care of your body. It's the only place you have to live".

Jim Rohn

~4~

Shifting Dimensions and Our Divine Consciousness

"We are near waking when we dream we are dreaming."
Novalis

As the world changes, our dimensions are shifting. We are entering a lighter, less dense period of physical reality, and regaining our old lost ability to shift dimensions intentionally. But until we once again take control of the process, we are randomly flipping through dimensions. A decade or so ago, the density of the planet was such that most of us were grounded in the third dimension. This is not true anymore. We have shifted, and with that shift comes new awareness and responsibility.

As we move into the higher dimensions, it is important that we become responsible for more of our own thoughts and behavior. In the third dimension, the density makes it more difficult to manifest on the physical plane. This slowness acted as a protection from our own lower thinking and acting. It protected us from ourselves.

As we move into the higher dimensions, our thoughts become our reality much faster and we are experiencing our own thoughts much quicker. This is the law of attractions and it is greatly sped up in the higher frequencies. We are forced to take responsibility for our creations and the karmic consequences.

As frequency and dimensions shift, the forces that once protected us from the consequences of our own thoughts and behaviors are being removed. We are being forced to be more aware and more responsible. We are also being forced to face and eliminate old habits, thoughts, and beliefs that are no longer in alignment with our higher selves.

As our vibrations and dimensions accelerate, we are no longer anchored in the solidarity of the third dimension. We are moving from third to the fourth to fifth and even to the sixth dimension. With each shift our reality changes. These dimensional shifts can be exhilarating or terrifying, depending on your perspective. These dimensional shifts may bring on new feelings and symptoms such as disorientation, foggy mind, and memory loss. These symptoms can cause people to react in different ways. How do you react?

Do you beat yourself up?

Blame your age, diet, or thoughts for being defective?

Do you sometimes feel depressed, anxious, and helpless?

Some people even blame others and thus strike out against what they perceive as an unfriendly world (think the rise of mass violence and shootings, epidemic levels of depression and anxiety, and the feeling of being stuck). The greater your level of awareness, balance, and trust in yourself, the less severe will be your experiences.

The shifting dimensions can feel much like waking up from a dream…there may be disorientation, brain fog, and memory loss. It often takes a minute to sort out physical reality from the dream reality. It takes a bit to orientate and gain balance in your new world as you leave the old dream world.

Now imagine bouncing between your dream state and awake state. Imagine you have no control over the process. You can't even predict when it will happen. Now how will you feel? How confused would you be? Who would you blame? What strategies would you use to anchor in one state or the other? Would you even try...or would you just curse yourself for being crazy?

This shifting from dream to awake is much like what shifting in and out of the dimensions feels like. Even though "nothing" has changed; your orientation, thoughts, beliefs and mental processes differ greatly. If you don't trust your own sanity, you can feel like you are losing your mind.

Have you experienced any of this? Are you interested in learning more? Then keep reading...

"We misuse language and talk about the 'ascent' of man. We understand the scientific basis for the interrelatedness of life, but our ego hasn't caught up yet".

Jill Tarter

~5~

The Third Dimension

"In order to more fully understand this reality, we must take into account other dimensions of a broader reality."
John Archibald Wheeler

Until recently (at least through the 1950's), most humans existed in the third dimension. This existence is characterized by the basic physical perceptions. In the third dimension, humanity believes that what is real (and thus important) is what can be seen, heard, tasted, smelled, and touched. The five physical senses dictate what is *real*. Humanity believes what is real in their physical life is filled with physical sensations and input given through these senses.

Beliefs are formed as a result of experience. Life is viewed through physical eyes. The quality of physical stuff determines worth and success. Spoken words and other outside influences often determine personal mood. This is the most basic third-dimensional conscious reality. The outer physical reality is a reflection of the conscious awareness of the individual. What is real and important is on the outside of them.

In a third-dimensional reality, you are aware of only what can be touched, tasted, smelled, seen and heard. These things are real, but nothing else. Things that cannot be touched, tasted, smelled, seen, or heard are not real.

If I were to tell a third-dimensional reality-based person about how angels are helping all those who allow it, they might laugh or want to lock me away because that person would think angels are not real. If I told that same person that someone could read his/her mind, he would not believe it because, from the person's dimensional perspective, mind reading is silly, evil, or impossible.

At the most basic level of third-dimensional consciousness, a person sees himself as a victim of life, helpless to influence it in even the most basic of ways. He believes that he merely functions and survives. He may call on God to intervene on his behalf because he believes he has no power. For the person who is at this level, life on Earth may not be very fun. He sees himself as a feather being blown about by the winds of life. He feels he is a victim of everyone else's reality.

Many people functioning in the third dimension often do not believe in the existence of God because there is no *proof* that He exists. Until they have tangible proof, they cannot believe. A little higher on this third dimension frequency scale would be the third-dimensional people who accept God's existence. But this God must be patterned after their third-dimensional world. If they held religious beliefs they would be physical in nature. Heaven is a place. God is human-like and exists in some physical-type form. Every spiritual belief would have some sort of a third-dimensional form to be considered real. Everything operates on a physical model even though it is outside the visual range.

Their God is a human-like being who punishes the bad and rewards the good. This God punishes them when they do something wrong and rewards them when they do something right.

For example, they believe in situations like, "Because I did something wrong, God burned down my house," or "I was kind to an old lady, so God allowed me to win the lottery." They see poverty as a direct result of a person's bad deeds and abundance as God's reward. This concept of God is dictated by their reality. Therefore, God exists as a person-type being who lives in heaven, a wonderful place to visit somewhere just beyond the stars (take a left at Saturn), but the believer has to die first. If you mismanage your life, you go to hell (take a right at Saturn and drink plenty of water).

At the highest level of the third dimension, a person would begin to release the need to have a person-type God and allow a greater variety of form. He would begin to see God as the Creator of diversity and therefore be diverse in its own existence. But God is still separate and outside him. "I am here, and God is in heaven." *It is the __separateness__ that earmarks the third dimension and third-dimensional reality.*

At the outermost reaches of a third-dimensional frequency, a slight awareness emerges of a reality greater than the five senses can perceive. At this level, people become curious about what cannot be seen, tasted, touched, heard, or smelled—like astrology, paranormal topics, and psychic phenomena. (At the most basic third-dimensional level, all of these would be ridiculed or condemned.) As the dimensional awareness shifts, one might begin to read the astrology section of the paper for entertainment (but it wouldn't be believed), or a psychic might be visited—just for the fun of it. A ghost hunting trip might be planned on a lark. The fourth dimension is beginning to nibble into reality.

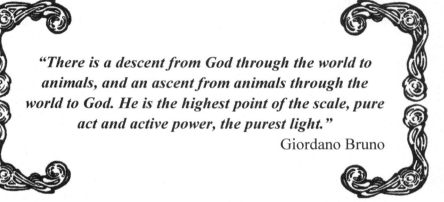

"There is a descent from God through the world to animals, and an ascent from animals through the world to God. He is the highest point of the scale, pure act and active power, the purest light."

Giordano Bruno

~6~

Fourth Dimension

"We each have a sixth sense that is attuned to the oneness dimension in life, providing a means for us to guide our lives in accord with our ideas."

Henry Reed

The third dimension has clear firm rules. The fifth dimension has clear firm rules. The fourth dimension doesn't. It was designed to be the cushion and provide a time for transition between third and fifth dimension.

If we use a travel analogy to illustrate dimensions, then 3D would be New York, and 5D would be Los Angeles. The journey between NY and LA would be the fourth dimension. Everybody is taking this trip, you don't have a choice.

The third dimension is defined by our 5 physical senses. What is real; can be tasted, smelled, felt, heard, and seen. Real things are always not something else. There is separation and is defined by duality. I can feel where the TV starts and I can feel where the TV stops. I can see where the table starts and where it ends. I can feel a book on a shelf. I experience the separation. That separation is what defines third dimension and it is designed to create duality. We recognize good and bad, right and wrong, up and down. Almost everything has a duality based on separation.

If we go to the other extreme and examine 5D i.e., California, it is defined by unity. We see the oneness. We no longer feel a separation but instead, we experience oneness. Fifth dimension is defined by that recognition that we are all one, and the greater ability to experience more light, to be more accepting, to be more honoring, to be more in peace, to be more in harmony. It's really what we all want in our lives.

But if humanity tried to go from 3D to 5D, it would literally blow the mind. So there had to be a time of transition. Fourth dimension provides the opportunity to make the journey from third and fifth dimension. That's why we don't hear a lot about fourth dimension. Fourth dimension is the search state, it's what happens between third and fifth, and each dimension has degrees. It is the releasing of the mind's hold on your experiences. It is a time of search and exploration. You can be in 3D one minute and 5D another. You may be a little bit in third, a little bit in fifth, and you volley back and forth.

Fourth dimension is a time of searching for reality; it signals openness to things unseen . . . to things not perceived by the five senses. Fourth dimension becomes the reality that operates beyond the five senses. It is marked by questions…you want to know THE TRUTH! You are beginning to recognize that the five senses do not mark the edge of the universe.

Indeed, as your vibrational frequency is increased so too is the dimensional reality that is perceived. At the fourth dimension, people begin to recognize the control they have over their lives and begin to take more responsibility for their world.

The fourth dimension mandates that individuals become aware of, and responsible for, how they create the circumstances of their own life and they are not a victim of them. They realize they are living in a cause-and-effect world; people become aware that they are responsible for their world and everything in it. In the security of the third dimension, one does not assume responsibility; instead, one can blame the rest of the world for one's personal life challenges, but in fourth dimension, this truth cannot be ignored.

Often people expect great changes as they move into the fourth dimension, but it doesn't happen like that. It is simply a gradual awakening to new possibilities and finally to the new reality that there is more to this life than can be seen, heard, smelled, touched, and tasted. No lightning bolts from heaven or major life adjustments occur. The fourth dimension is not "out there," but within the perceptual reality of each person, waiting to emerge.

In the third dimension everything that is important is on the outside of a person, but as the reality of fourth-dimensional existence begins to emerge, you realize that what is really important is on the inside.

This is what my spirit friends shared with me, *"The fourth dimension, although simple in nature, is very complicated for the mortal mind to grasp. It is what people experience in the dream state. It is a dimension beyond the physical; it is of the energy spirits. It is the hearing of what is not there. It is knowing what can't be known. It is what many can already do, but trust it not because it is not "normal." But soon it will be normal. Now is the time of a great awakening to the vastness of life. It is a moving beyond the limits of the physical. It is the knowing of the joy of angels. It is recognizing oneness with "All-That-Is. It is a glorious time! Prayer, light, and love will allow you to move into this new awareness without struggle or resistance."*

People still functioning at the third-dimensional level are threatened by those who venture outside the safety of the third dimension. The say the devil will get you. God will forsake you. You will go to hell for questioning. They pray for your soul. They do everything they can to get you to turn back to the safety of the good solid third dimension. Just remember, your journey is your choice!

As people search for truth, they will move into 4D reality. They begin to realize that there is something greater than physical existence. They begin to know that some things cannot be seen, heard, touched, smelled, or tasted but exist nevertheless. As they begin to realize a connection exists between themselves and other worlds, they begin to search out these other existences. They will find evidence of these other worlds through their channel of perception. The three most common senses through which people find proof are hearing, seeing, and feeling without ears, eyes, or fingers.

Clairaudience is the hearing of sounds, music, and voices not audible to normal hearing. This French term means "clear hearing." It is not a new phenomenon. Oracles, priests, mystics, shamans, adepts, saints, prophets and holy persons through the ages have recorded occurrences of clairaudient experiences. A few decades ago, if people spoke of hearing voices, they would be locked away—perhaps forever—because they were considered abnormal or insane. Even being locked away was infinitely better than being burned at the stake as a witch—a typical punishment just a few hundred years ago. Even Joan of Arc, whose voices saved the French and proved to be correct in every way, was eventually burned at the stake for hearing voices.

Bless Joan, and others like her, for standing in her truth! They gave us a model of courage that we may still need to call upon.

As more stable, intelligent, sincere, and honest people begin to admit to hearing these disembodied voices, their reality can no longer be denied. Some of these voices, either internal or external, will be accepted as conversations with off-planet beings and/or other dimensional beings. (For more information on this, read my book, ***Interdimensional Communication).***

These voices are clearly distinguishable from human ones. Many well-known people have heard voices that guided them to greatness.

> Socrates claimed to be guided by a spirit friend throughout his life. When sentenced to death, he willingly drank the poison because his guide did not advise him to do otherwise.

> King Solomon, as well as several other Bible characters, admitted to hearing voices.

> Joan of Arc led armies by the advice of her spirit friends.

> George Washington was said to decide battle strategies based on visits from his angelic helpers.

> Even Abe Lincoln credits his success in the Civil War with advice he received from his spiritual sources.

Clairvoyants see into other dimensions. Clear seeing or perceiving objects, events, or people that cannot be perceived by the physical eye, is relatively common. Some people see the forms outside themselves like visions, whereas others have an internal vision like mental movies.

For some people, the simplest type of clairvoyance is an internal sight of symbolic images which must be interpreted. In its highest form, one looks into the various dimensions and sees directly.

Nostradamus, the French psychic, is said to have this type of clairvoyance.

Many people have reported different types of clairvoyance. Some tell of being able to see through things like envelopes and walls. Some are able to see disease and illness in the energy field of the body or the aura. Some can see faraway events and/or people. Still, others are able to see beyond time and space. All are normal and occur frequently as the people move into fourth-dimensional reality.

Clairsentience, or clear sensing, is a nonphysical sense perception. It is *feeling* the information but not with fingers. It may come as a fleeting impression, a brief image, intuition, or a gut reaction. These may register as internal or external impressions. People experience many forms of clairsentience.

The experience is similar to, yet stronger than, intuition. It can often be described as a soft idea, only much stronger and clearer. The more people attend to this knowing, the stronger and clearer it gets and the more confident and trusting they will become with it.

Clairsentience, clairvoyance, and clairaudience are not skills attached to an on/off switch. They are not an either you have them or you don't experience. Instead, they represent a continuum of fourth-dimensional realities. All people have the potential for these abilities. In some people they lie dormant, never to be used. But for others, they are recognized and used freely. These extrasensory abilities change, enhance, and expand the quality of their life.

Things can and do exist beyond what can be seen, touched, heard, tasted, and smelled by the physical body. As people move into a fourth-dimensional consciousness, they **know** and accept this as their truth. In the fourth dimension, a person recognizes that life is a play; he or she is the starring actor, the playwright, and the casting director. If a terrible mother or a dreadful father has been written into their life script and he/she is tired of playing that role or wants to stop working with that character, he/she knows they have the ability to rewrite the script. By changing themselves, they have the power to change everything . . . and they know it.

In the fourth dimension, no longer can people say, "Oh, poor me, I just don't have any money this week," or "I don't have . . . "instead they ask, "Why did I do that to myself? What is the lesson I need to learn?"

When someone indescribably bad comes into their life, they ask themselves, "What is that person trying to teach me?" "Why did I draw them into my life?"

The third-dimensional reality is fear and separation-based, whereas the fourth dimension is the transition phase where they begin to take control of their life and life circumstances. This is an important step toward choosing love. Love is the single element that defines the fifth dimension. As people recognize that all things are within their power to control and that love brings harmony to all things, they move easily from the fourth to the fifth-dimensional consciousness. It becomes their choice to move into the unifying power of love.

In the fourth dimension, the concept of God expands. No longer is God someone who punishes or rewards. God is no longer a human-like being who sits on a throne but becomes a figureless spiritual essence which permeates everything. God is the higher power, infinite intelligence, and the creator of all things.

Many people operating at the fourth dimension realize that the God Essence is a part of all, and all are part of the God Essence. The merging of the self and the Godness begins. God moves from a separate outside figure to a presence that is everywhere and can be found within the heart as easily as in a temple, cathedral, church, or mosque.

In the fourth dimension, people begin to accept all things as wonderful opportunities for growth. This acceptance is the being of unconditional love into their daily lives. They begin to realize that only through unconditional love can they fully attain their Human greatness and claim their power, not as an outer force but as an inner state. They become ***empowered***.

The fourth dimension is the transitional state of awareness from where we were (third dimension) to where we are going (fifth dimension). It is in this transition phase which requires that we release all third-dimensional truths and be open to divine truth. The fourth dimension is most noted for its sacred search for truth. As we search for truth, what we desire to know slowly takes shape. The answers aren't found in the fourth dimension, but the questions which will lead to the answers are formulated here.

~7~

Fifth Dimension

"There is a fifth dimension, beyond that which is known to man. It is a dimension as vast as space and as timeless as infinity. It is the middle ground between light and shadow, between science and superstition."

Rod Serling

In the fifth dimension, the answer to all our questions becomes apparent. The solutions to all our problems are made clear.

Love is everything. Love is all we need.

Love—not the kissy-huggy type of love so programmed into humanity—but the deep, unconditional, all-accepting, unifying kind of love is the answer. Love seems too clear and simple that it is hard to understand why it was ever in doubt.

The fifth dimension is marked by the unity and the realization that we are all one. Truth emerges bubbling up from our center. "Nothing, or no one, is separate from the whole." What affects one, affects all. The Golden Rule, "Do unto others as you would have them do unto you," takes on a deeper meaning. Action towards others changes and become more intentional. People begin to live mindfully present in the moment. Consequences of possible actions are carefully considered before action is taken.

The fifth dimension is about total surrender to the God Essence or soul/spirit. Which word you chose is not important because the spirit/self is directly connected to the God Source. The act of surrender to divine will is significant for it represents relinquishing control to the forces of unconditional love or higher consciousness.

In the fifth-dimensional consciousness, humanity realizes there is so much more to humans than meets the eye (or the other five senses) and willingly learns to "pull in" the greater part of who they are into their lives. Through this process, people learn to harmonize their individual frequency with the vibrations of the higher forces.

In the fourth dimension, people know there is more to life. They just don't exactly know what it is. In the fourth dimension, they must make the challenging journey from the head (knowing it) to heart (living it). In fifth dimension, heart-felt must be lived.

The fifth dimension brings unconditional love and acceptance in their daily life. They experience a unity with the God Essence. This dimensional reality does not accept the concept of a punishing, demanding, or rewarding God. People existing in the fifth dimension would never humble themselves before God because, in their new understanding, they recognize that God would not find that behavior acceptable.

This God would want humanity to come with heads held high to accept the gifts of abundance from a loving God who is gender free and form free. They realize that they have inherited all the gifts of God and thus have the power to create the life they choose to live. Their God would never want nor expect subservience or an arbitrary perfection in humanity. Rather, it is understood that this God would want someone with a loving and pure heart who wishes to continue to grow and ascend to higher and higher levels. Divine perfection is clear and understood as being the standard which accepts and unconditionally loves all of humanity. This fifth-dimensional human recognizes the Godness in all things and in all people.

The divine "God" is not changing; rather, the human understanding and definition of the Divine are being altered. Just as if we asked a child to define a father, his definition would doubtless change and mature as he grew older, so too the definition of "God" is altered with each new dimensional level and understanding.

The fifth-dimensional God Essence is a force that unifies and binds all things together. In the fifth dimension, people recognize they are not separate from the God Essence but are part of the greater whole. They no longer look for God outside themselves in a place called Heaven but recognize that God dwells within them. To find God requires an inward journey; to know God requires a person to know him/herself and to know him/herself is to know God. All are one in the fifth dimension awareness. The God Essence is seen as the great Creator who endowed humanity with the ability to co-create. A fifth-dimensional person would never violate this great gift. Earth-based volunteers recognize that their creative nature continually creates with every thought, word, and deed. Creation is not just an intentional act but a continuous act that cannot be stopped. At this level of understanding, Humanity must acknowledge that every aspect of their life is of their own making.

People in the fifth-dimensional consciousness experience the truth that all are one. There is no separation. All pain is their pain; all hurt is their hurt. All joy is their joy. What happens to a little puppy on the street also happens to them. They know that all things impact them, and they impact all things. Humans who have achieved the fifth-dimensional level know and show compassion as few others can.

Compassion becomes a living component in their life. They feel for everything. They have compassion for their food, neighbors, even those people who do them wrong.

Many children who function in a fifth-dimensional state of consciousness feel the pain of the world. Well-intended adults often assure them that it is only their imagination, but it does little good. These children feel a powerful connection to all, so it is hard for them to understand how adults can pass by without noticing, feeling, or caring. The world is very confusing to them.

All conscious separation ends in the fifth dimension. Groups come together for the greater good. These groups focus on the common good and build on common ground. In the third dimension, group members see differences. In the fifth dimension, commonality is seen. The difference still exists but it is handled very differently.

Competition is replaced with cooperation and collaboration, which creates group harmony. The art of collaboration is more important than being the Lone Ranger and going it alone. Relationships are very important in the fifth dimension. Relations are neither personal nor emotional, but transpersonal/impersonal. People acknowledge their relationship with all living things—the animal, plant, and mineral kingdoms, the Earth, the moon, the air, the oceans, the universe, to name just a few. Many Native Americans understood and lived those relationships to the fullest.

People recognize, at this fifth-dimensional state, the existence of the extraterrestrials. Contacts and involvement with brothers and sisters of space take on new expressions. Meeting their Cosmic Cousins is a matter of when and not if. People know and know they know, this existence is not just on this planet, in this physical space, but is made up of many universes and types of existences. They don't need proof because they know and know that they know. They look forward to meeting their cosmic cousins. For they know all are part of the family of God. They trust that when that time comes, they will be able to discern the intentions of others and will know how to react to them. They recognize free will allows individuals of all life forms to choose when to serve the greater good or their own agendas.

At their core, humans know there are people who work for the good of the planet and others who work for its control and domination of humanity. This is not judged nor embraced—only acknowledged as expressions of the realities of others. It is at this frequency that the conscious mind allows access to the greater wisdom which contains an awareness of off-planet activity, other lifetimes in service, and other planetary experiences. At this point, many volunteers move into their total personal power and commitment to the greater service.

Making the transition to the fifth dimension can be smooth and without difficulty, or it can be just the opposite. Surrender to your new awareness or fight it, your choice. But at some point, you may not have a choice about making the change. The collective, dimensional consciousness on the Earth is affected by the combined frequencies of the individual Earth-based volunteers: as one is raised, so is the other. The collective vibrational frequency of the planet is continually being raised. People will either resist the frequency and cause themselves great discomfort, or they will accept this greater vibrational reality and make the transition easily. Relax, allow, and pray to know and accept the truth.

For most of the people living on this planet, the dimensional journey stops with the fifth dimension. But there are dimensions beyond this fifth dimension. With each higher, they are increasingly more challenging to define and describe.

> *"In any case, in so far as our knowledge of the universe carries us, the advent of civilization for the first time on our globe represents the highest ascent of the life processes to which evolution had anywhere attained."*
>
> James Henry Breasted

~8~

Sixth Dimension

"All things are connected like the blood that unites us. We do not weave the web of life, we are merely a strand in it. Whatever we do to the web, we do to ourselves."

Chief Seattle

In each higher dimension, the former reality gives way to a greater awareness. All beliefs are laid open for examination and reexamination. Old issues must be processed anew and brought to closure. The issues repressed in lower dimensions rise to the surface until they are resolved.

As the vibrational frequency ascends to the sixth-dimensional level, what is significant is found in sounds, symbols, and tones. Oneness is assumed.

Language becomes less and less important. The limitation of words becomes apparent.

In fifth dimension, growth occurs through our interactions with others. But in sixth dimension, growth is often a product of inward work stimulated by outer perceptions. A flash of understanding, a meaningful pictograph, a symbolic crop circle can cause great change that defies words.

As volunteers move into the sixth-dimensional level, they begin to understand why they had to break up old beliefs and why they were unable to use language to express their new conscious reality. They are able to know volumes, often in a flash that would take hours to convert into words—if it were even possible to find words to convey the meaning. A sixth-dimensional being has great difficulty explaining to a third-dimensional person what this dimension is because it is beyond language.

Human heart-to-heart connection doesn't happen with words; it is a presence that exists between them. Intimacy, so important to life, is nearly impossible to experience in third-dimensional consciousness because the core 3-D belief rests in isolation and separation. In the sixth dimension, consciousness simply is. Life exists in such a state of intimacy that it is hard to imagine any other way. Vulnerability is understood as the core of invincibility, not something to avoid.

In sixth dimension, people recognize the wasted energy that words represent. Words become less and less capable of expressing humanity's knowings. No words exist to express these new insights and truth. These indescribable events are the signals of the journey into the sixth dimension, but those who do understand need no words and those that don't cannot possibly understand—no matter what is said.

Sixth dimension is similar to what happens to a person in his dream state where he experiences kaleidoscopic-type experiences that weave in and out. The dream made sense as it was dreamed but trying to explain it to another person is impossible.

At the sixth-dimensional level exists a reality of symbolism. There is still the world of physicality as it is currently experienced on Earth, but reality is not defined by it. All the lessons of the lower dimensions are simply expanded into a new awareness.

In the sixth dimension, there are new colors and lights and music and exquisite beauty. The one who is transformed sees the world around him with new eyes in a new state of awareness.

When Earth-based volunteers move into a sixth-dimensional frequency, although they may say very little, they assist others with their very presence to move more quickly out of third dimension into fourth or out of fourth into fifth. Just by radiating the higher frequency, they impact those around them. Others feel their own cellular evolution and acceleration in the presence of a person who has achieved sixth-dimensional consciousness.

Mother Earth and most of those in residence on this Earth are not yet ready for such a pure sixth-dimensional frequency but individuals with sixth-dimensional frequency help accelerate the planet into the fifth dimension, which is the vibration that Earth will embrace after the Earth's transformation is complete. This indeed is the mission and the reason for the Earth-based volunteers. For this reason, many Earth-based volunteers are drawn to such things as symbols, mantras, tones, music, sacred mathematics, and pictographic-type symbols. If properly used, these can assist people to awaken to higher realities. They are flashes into the sixth-dimensional world.

If a grounded 3-D person looks at a particular image they experience nothing. If a fifth-dimensional person views the same image they "get it," although they will not be able to tell you what they get.

Volunteers must be careful, however, not to become dependent on anything including forms, symbols, or tones outside of themselves.

The power is within them and is not found in things. These items are tools that can help but never substitute for conscious, directed thought at the higher frequencies. For instance, a hammer is a useful tool, but it does not define the carpenter. It is the carpenter who determines whether or not the hammer will be used for construction or destruction: good or harm.

Mathematics originated in the sixth dimension. When you truly understand the principles behind mathematics, you are in touch with great forces. Many people perceive Einstein and others of his intellectual equal as being able to go beyond physical reality, and they were. That is why he, and others like him, broke the traditional view of reality and talked of probabilities which other people did not normally address. These people were not born greater than any other; they merely turned inward and thus became great.

People who reach this level often choose to disassociate themselves from many typical human activities, for those activities no longer serve any purpose to them. In the sixth dimension, they work solely for the good of all; the individual is of little significance. Others are valued above the self.

In a sixth-dimensional reality, the physical body loses its significance; therefore, for the most part, it does not play a part in the human growth experience because it is not an important part of reality. The lessons of the physical body have been mastered. The human consciousness knows to program health into every cell. Eating, sleeping and other physical needs become secondary.

People who achieve the highest sixth-dimensional frequency may appear or disappear at will. They have mastered and broken through the limitation of physical existence. They are able to adjust their physical vibration at will, allowing them to appear or disappear. Think of a fan, if you look at it at different speeds you will see different images. When the blades of the fan spin slowly, you may see them as separate blades or even as a disk. Turn the speed of the fan up and the disk may disappear completely. As dimensional-aware individuals, they too learn to adjust the vibratory levels of their bodies. At the highest levels, they disappear completely. This is the highest use of the physical body. You can turn up or down the vibratory level at will. You have mastered the physical body. It no longer dictates your experience.

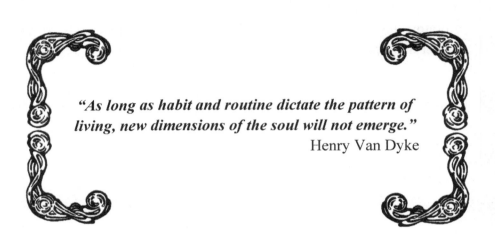

"As long as habit and routine dictate the pattern of living, new dimensions of the soul will not emerge."

Henry Van Dyke

~9~

Seventh Dimension

"A mind that is stretched by a new experience can never go back to its old dimensions."

Oliver Wendell Holmes, Jr.

In the seventh dimension, there is no longer a need for a physical body. The need for physical confinement or limitation no longer exists. There are no further lessons to learn from the body; therefore, it is left behind. You still have a unique, seventh-dimensional form. Perhaps it would be a spirit form or light body or perhaps an expression of color, sound, or tone. The individuality of the entity still exists—much like a drop in the ocean. Those who exist in the seventh-dimensional totality of creation know who they are and are aware of their unique individuation of existence even though nothing actually separates the individual from the entirety.

In this seventh-dimensional consciousness, one learns lessons of unique expression outside the limitations of physical form. While in a body much of one's individual nature is defined by the body, but in the seventh dimension, one learns about his unique nature in other ways. The focus of seventh dimension is on inward growth and outward expression of it.

It is a state of connection with Divine Source and well beyond the limits of language. One knows all because of the quality and clarity of one's connection with *All That Is*. The goal is to learn to work in perfect synchronization with the Divine. Like two professional dancers who have danced together for eons so too does a seventh-dimensional being learn to move in perfect union with the Divine. Issues of honesty and integrity have been long mastered; the goal at this level is to move in perfect harmony with *All That Is*.

You lose yourself and your need for separation in the joy of the divine union. It is a total state of surrender.

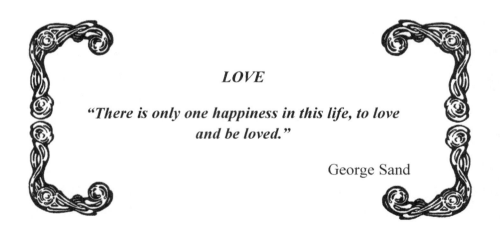

LOVE

"There is only one happiness in this life, to love and be loved."

George Sand

~10~

Eighth Dimension

"Life is a journey that must be traveled no matter how bad the roads and accommodations."

Oliver Goldsmith

Beyond the seventh dimension, there is only the universal, the collective, the mass. There is no longer specific individual process or form. You feel the unity because you *are* the unity. Those at this level exist in the ebb and tide of universal flow. At this level, there is no separateness between one drop of water in the ocean and the ocean. You are one with all but you are aware of what you are within that whole.

The eighth dimension is void of form as we know it because no form exists or is needed. The sound of the universe rings constantly (though felt, not heard). It is similar to that which is heard in a large seashell. Beings experience the flow of the universe in this dimension. All are a part of *All That Is,* but it is recognized that there are still new experiences in consciousness.

All consciousness swirls like ocean tides. No separation exists, yet beings are aware of their influencing presence. Just as a committee is formed on the Earth to define larger purposes, so do individuals willingly give up individuality to experience collective awareness.

The best analogy may be found in getting tasks done. It is usually much easier and faster just to do the job alone… rather than having a committee attempt to perform the same task. It takes more effort to get the committee working together for a common purpose. However, if the committee works together long enough and works in unison of purpose well enough, the completion of the job becomes easier.

So it is with eighth dimension. In the beginning, it is difficult to work in conscious union with others; but as the evolution of spirit takes place, it becomes much easier. In the beginning, perhaps a dozen or so combine consciousnesses; but at the highest level of eighth dimension, thousands upon thousands can be in perfect union.

(This gets a little mind bending…so brace yourself.) To test their harmonious unions, this eighth-dimensional collection of consciousness can or may choose a third-dimensional physical body in order to experience life in the physical as a single expression. If it is done well, the physical being is a wealth of knowledge and capabilities as none of the wisdom or skills of the individual consciousnesses are lost in the merging union. This eighth-dimensional being may be recognized as a genius with amazing and varied talent. A talented dancer, artist, scientist, explorer, inventor, and writer may all be found in one person in one lifetime.

However, if things are not so harmoniously unified, a being with incredible internal conflict is created. Constantly tormented and torn between multiple goals and competing interests creates a human life of internal torture. Multiple personalities or consciousnesses that compete for time and attention can result. These are labeled personality disorders or mental illness when in truth, they are soul consciousness discordance and distortions of the highest order. The mind which is often blamed for these disturbances is but the pawn in an internal power struggle.

From the eighth dimension, group consciousness exists as a single manifestation. Perhaps like a group of friends who are very close and who decide to unite for a common purpose. These collective, eighth-dimensional consciousness literally become one essence that contains the attribute of all the entities involved.

Eight-dimensional reality is a kind of marriage of spirits. The marriage can work in many ways, including choosing a physical form to act as an ambassador on Earth for this eighth-dimensional group consciousness. (For the record, any dimensional being can choose to come back to Earth in a physical body to test their own abilities and soul growth.) Nothing is lost, but only combined; the group synergy creates a much vaster reality and soul growth experience.

As you move up through the frequency dimensions, the element of separation that is so important in the third and fourth-dimensional life is gradually eliminated by the increasing awareness that separation itself is the illusion upon which the lower frequencies are based. Purification of the individual becomes much more important until, at this level, the individual is no longer necessary.

In the eighth dimension, the method of increased unity occurs. This is the unifying of collective groups with larger and larger groups. When communicating with other dimensions, those communications refer to themselves as "we" when asked, "Who is there?" The "we" represents a much larger unit of consciousness.

These consciousness units continue to grow until they represent hundreds of thousands of combined individual souls/spirits. This is but a phase of preparation as one moves up the dimensional realities. The ultimate purpose is unification with the God Consciousness in a totality of perception. Feeling increasingly comfortable with losing their individual identity (seventh dimension), various individuals' energies see the need to come together and combine with like consciousness to create a greater whole.

Many lessons are learned in each dimension, but the eighth dimension prepares the way for total unification with *All That Is*. As a group consciousness moves beyond the need for lessons and growth at this level, it moves into ninth-dimensional consciousness.

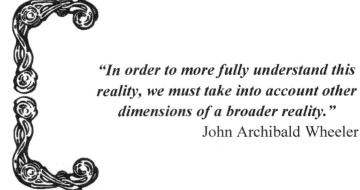

"In order to more fully understand this reality, we must take into account other dimensions of a broader reality."
John Archibald Wheeler

~11~

Ninth Dimension

"Do the difficult things while they are easy and do the great things while they are small. A journey of a thousand miles must begin with a single step."

Lao Tzu

In the ninth dimension, group consciousnesses choose to come together en masse to manifest as learning environments for the growth of others in the form of planets, galaxies, stars, or universes. They create a much greater collective reality. In essence, they are collections of collective consciousnesses and become an environment in which other beings at various dimensional levels continue their growth. Much like university professors might come together to design and create a laboratory school in which they learn by observing children function in a classroom. The laboratory allows people to learn by observing the behaviors of others. Scientists create and provide a learning environment for laboratory animals in order to observe them in a natural state. They do this so they can learn from the learning experience of their subjects. In both of these examples, others learn by observing those in residence in their intentionally designed learning environments.

Ninth dimensional consciousnesses function much like these laboratories which they themselves create. They learn and evolve by providing an environment in which others learn, grow and evolve.

Many consciousnesses combined in the eighth dimension to learn to work in harmony; but in the ninth dimension, these combinations grow exponentially and put themselves in service for the greater good of others. They see the importance of the greater reality, so they offer themselves as an opportunity for growth. This is the ultimate experience of unconditional love and unselfish service.

Earth is a ninth dimensional consciousness being who has provided a unique experience for those in residence. Earth learns and grows as a result of our individual and collective decisions. She learns through the behavior of those in residence.

Each learning environment and there are millions, determines and serves a unique learning environment. Earth teaches us about free will. Here we learn how to live with the consequences of our thoughts.

Each dimension comes with a "serving mindset" but the motivation and reasons may vary. At the third-dimensional level, people may help others because they feel the need to fix or heal them. (Third-dimensional thinking says you are either broken or you are well.)

In fourth-dimensional reality, individuals offer aid or help only when asked. (They are beginning to recognize the power of free will and do not want to interfere without being asked.)

At the fifth dimension, one feels little need to interfere with the life experiences of others because one recognizes the growth opportunities they contain. (They serve others by bathing them in love and empowering them to be able to heal themselves.)

No interference of any kind would occur in the sixth, seventh or eighth dimensions.

In ninth dimensional reality, one gives himself totally into service for the growth opportunities of others because no perceived differences exist between self and "others." Never is growth forced upon another; new opportunities are offered to those who wish to continue their growth. With the present Earth concept of matter, time and space, it is difficult to conceive that Mother Earth is such a unit of consciousness.

Earth is a beloved ninth dimensional being who has given freely of herself in order to provide growth opportunities for those who choose to experience her unique gifts. Earth is a sentient being who is as alive as we humans. Like a dog who provides an environment for fleas, fleas can determine the dog's health and comfort level. We humans also determine the health of this planet and thus far, we aren't doing so well at keeping her healthy. (Read more about this in my book, *__Many Were Called, Few Were Chosen: the Story of Mother Earth and the Earth-based Volunteers__*).

Do you have children? If you do, you know that you have been learning from them from the moment they were born. Even as the child grows from dependence to independence they are both learning and teaching along the way. The parents who have conceived the child continue to grow through and from their child's experience. Acting as their mother is a sacred title.

We use that same sacred title on this planet. She is often referred to as Mother Earth as we recognize this Earth gave us the opportunity of life. Ninth-dimensional beings (Earth and other like her) are often identified by the honored title of "Mother" because of their life-giving nature.

Again, the growth opportunities afforded by a ninth dimensional consciousness is a living laboratory designed to be a learning environment in which others experience and grow. Thus, Mother Earth learns by experiencing the growth and behavior of those in residence.

Each ninth dimensional consciousness offers new opportunities. When Mother Earth moved into existence, her gift was the gift of free will. This incredible and unique gift was only offered on this planet. No other planet in all of the universes and universes beyond universes has ever offered people the opportunity to experience the manifestation of their unlimited free will choice. Therefore, planet Earth offers a diversity of form found nowhere else.

Every thought could become manifested. Unlimited choice with unlimited consequences was an amazing and aggressive undertaking for a planet. Mother Earth was special, and so too were those who were brave enough to live and experience their own creations.

Individual free will was the gift and also the responsibility; each person had to stand accountable for his creations. Collective free will was also part of the free will experience. Each person stood accountable for his creations, and together people had to stand accountable for their collective actions.

In the beginning, physical density was one choice offered on Earth but you were not locked into it. Only when the vibrational frequency became so low that it could not support the free moving in and out of physical matter did people become trapped by their choices. Indeed, this was free will in action.

Unfortunately, when the extremely low vibrational frequencies occurred, humanity chose to embrace and experience fear, greed, judgment, hate, scarcity, duality, violence, and other such thoughts. These lowered the vibration even lower and caused, even more, challenge for Mother Earth. Certainly, humanity had the free will to make these choices, but no one expected humanity to repeatedly choose them over love, joy, harmony, peace, prosperity, happiness, and unity. As a result, Mother Earth was not prepared for the vibrational consequences of them. When humans could have their heart's desire, who would have guessed they would choose to live a nightmare of hate, violence, pain and suffering.

These extremely low frequencies mandated changes on this planet. It has also created the current state of health for the planet.

The change now being experienced on Mother Earth is the dimensional shift from third-dimensional (a lower slower vibrational frequency known for its density and duality) to a fifth-dimensional reality (a higher faster vibrational frequency of oneness). This is a major shift from humanity's identity based on duality and separateness to one of unity and love.

This shift must occur if the Mother Earth is to survive. The Earth-based volunteers known as lightworkers have come to help.

The shift will occur. The Lightworkers are here to act as midwives to the process. This can be a painless and relatively simple birth or one that requires much time and pain and causes much agony.

The act of choosing is free will in action and all on planet Earth will help decide. The more love, peace, harmony, gratitude and unity are chosen, the easier will be the shift.

Otherwise, great numbers of people will die in order for Mother Earth to live. As their vibrations, along with their lives, are taken from the planet, the vibrational shift of the planet will continue. A massive loss of life may/will occur in many ways. Earth changes, extreme weather, disease, and famine are a few ways that people will choose to evacuate the planet. Street violence, war, and terrorism will also claim the lives of those who still support duality. This is the fastest way to shift the energy vibration of the planet. Let those who hate, cheat, abuse, etc., die. Yes, there will be some others who may die as well, but just as in war sometimes there are innocent casualties. Every person that dies to save the planet has made a soul agreement to do so. Love is a much easier solution.

Earth changes and extreme weather always occur at points of lowest vibration. Love is a much easier solution.

Duality claims that one must die for another to live. It professes, as a core belief, that one must lose in order for another to win. As long as anyone on the planet believes this, force and violence will be used to overcome the perceived enemy. This belief must die for people to stop dying.

Humanity's reaction to the massive loss of life will determine the next step. (I highly recommend my book, ***Life's Last Frontier: The world of death, dying and letting go***.) If they open their heart with love, compassion and caring, they help raise the Earth's vibration and end the destruction. But if they curse the heavens and move into blame and bitterness, they increase the likelihood of greater destruction.

Regardless of the method used, in the end, the Earth transformation will occur. The transition from third to fifth dimension will happen. Beloved Mother Earth, who suffers now because of the vibrational choices of humanity, waits patiently for the outcome. Her life and future weigh in the balance.

Each thought, word, and deed chosen by every person living on Earth determine how long and how severe her pain will be. Decide now to choose love, peace, unity, forgiveness, and compassion, and in that choice, Mother Earth is gently healed. This is the true mission of each Earth-based volunteer and each Lightworker in all the universe and universes beyond universes.

Just in case you need an incentive…free will mandates that you must experience what you create. It's that old "reap what you sow" Karma thing. So when you decide to choose love, peace, unity, forgiveness, and compassion, you also experience more of that in your life. Choose to send loving thoughts and loving thoughts are sent to you.

For those willing to open their hearts to the whispering of Mother Earth, she has great wisdom to share. Please open your hearts now and hear her feelings.

This is a Message from Mother Earth to the Many Earth-Based Volunteers:
I feel the love that many of you send daily, and it acts like a tonic to my system. You, in turn, feel my pain and suffering, and it causes you great concern. Trust that we are connected by choice and that when you help yourself, you also help me for you have agreed to carry my burden. You have agreed to release me from the bondage of these lower frequencies. Do not judge another's perceptions or life experiences, as this causes you to also incur these lower frequencies. Because we are connected, I am affected by your choice.

Learn to trust your own source of greatness. Learn to allow the greater wisdom, which is a part of your own source of power, to guide your way. Trust your heart and soul to provide all that you need in this physical density. The way is not easy, but you did not expect it to be so when you volunteered. If you do all that you do in a light-filled and loving way, your Earth assignment can be shortened.

Some of you have lost your bearings. Lie on your belly and listen to my heart and feel my pulse. This will renew your sense of purpose and remembrance of your Earth mission. As you do this, ask All That Is to send love through you and into me. I need this and so do you.

You do not need to burn down the buildings of those who pollute my water because doing so causes more hate and fear and only serves to further my pain. They do not mean to destroy my existence, they operate out of fear—a fear of lack.

Teach all by example about how to bring in the light and how to live in the love vibration. Teach all how to move beyond fear and judgment. Teach all how to manifest all they need. I will teach you all that you need to know for this is my true nature. It is the reason for my existence. I want you to have it all.

You do not need to hoard my life blood which you call water. Ask me and I can give you all the clean, sparkling drink you want. Your loving thoughts can more than purify my water. You do not need to drain my lubricant to oil and run your motors. This makes my existence more uncomfortable—much like your dry skin.

Ask me and I will give you unlimited free power and technology. To receive all that you need and desire, you must first move into a state of responsibility for all. Move into your heart space. You must remember your Source, from which all comes. As science becomes heart-centered, and not ego or dollar-driven, answers will be given and shared freely with the world. There is enough for all.

I am ready, and so are you. I have existed long enough with lower frequencies of humanity's anger and fear. My vibrations have been held too low for too long through forces of destruction. Too many wars have been fought for silly reasons that have no meaning in the greater reality. Lift up thine eyes and see the light. The wisdom awaits you. I await you. Awaken to All That Is. Awaken to all that you are.

Mother Earth could choose death, for she too has choice. Death is simply a transformation from one form to another—even for a planet. If she were to give up her physical form, she would be free to choose another ninth dimensional existence. Or if she felt ready, she could move into a higher state of reality as a tenth-dimensional existence.

But she does not choose this. She wishes to continue to allow people to learn in this reality. Therefore, she fights for her very life; if she were to die, no other planet could or would replace her. The lessons learned on Earth would simply not be available to others.

The good news, there is a planet that has been prepared for those who die to reincarnate to that provides all the free will experiences of Earth but can handle the much denser choice of her residence. I was given the name of Ireon (Eye-re-on). This planet can handle the war, hate, greed, control, corruption, and other yucky stuff that humans are currently choosing. I certainly hope I don't have to experience that planet.

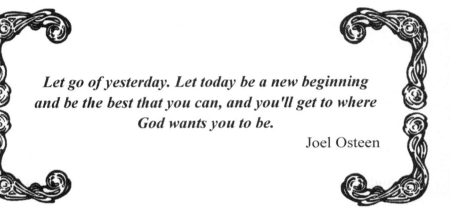

Let go of yesterday. Let today be a new beginning and be the best that you can, and you'll get to where God wants you to be.

Joel Osteen

~12~

Tenth Dimension and Beyond

"Evolution has ensured that our brains just aren't equipped to visualize 11 dimensions directly. However, from a purely mathematical point of view, it's as easy to think in 11 dimensions, as it is to think in three or four."

Stephen Hawking

Once a ninth dimension has completed its growth as a learning environment, it evolves into a tenth-dimensional being. The main function of a tenth-dimensional being is to help create and implement ninth dimensional environments. They are the master architects and builders of the planets (i.e. ninth dimensional learning environments).

Many tenth-dimensional beings who helped design this planet are now in human form as volunteers to help rescue her. (Yes, at any level dimensional beings can fragment into human form.) These tenth-dimensional beings may even suffer from great guilt since they did not create a safety net for their dear planet. None of them foresaw that when people could want for nothing, they would choose a life of want.

It was as if they built a Disneyland. Where people could come and live out every fantasy they dreamed of, and instead, people came to earth and chose to play in the toilet. Earth was designed as this breathtakingly beautiful planet, where people could choose anything. All they had to do was think on it and it would be theirs, yet they chose judgment, greed, hate, violence, and so much worse. They never saw it coming.

As far as Dimensions 11 & 12. The twelfth dimension is the soul's reunification with the Divine. This is the end of our soul's journey to experience itself as it once again becomes part of the magnificent divine *All That Is.*

From my perspective, these dimensions are beyond comprehension. As far as the Earth-based volunteers are concerned, these dimensions are not important at this time. I experienced them, they simply defy description. I must grow and evolve before I could begin to share my experience. For now, it is far more important to realize the great power of unconditional love and make its vibrational frequency is the basis of all that occurs in physical life.

As you have read of the dimensions, you have also brought the vibratory reality into your body. Feel how that feels in the physical body. Go back and read about them again and experience the energy. Breathe it in and let it flow through every cell.

The Earth-based volunteers have an important role to play on this beloved planet. It is time to awaken.

~13~

The Mind and Its Necessary Changes

"A mind that is stretched by a new experience can never go back to its old dimensions."

Oliver Wendell Holmes, Jr.

We have now examined on all the dimensions, now let's focusing on some of the changes that will occur as you move from third to the fifth dimension. What it means, and how it will impact you mentally and physically is important.

Many of the indications of our positive progress might be label "backslides," and even "yucky" because you are still judging your experience. It is my task to help you better understand these changes so you stop resisting and celebrate them…and thus speed your process.

Some of this is a review, but I feel it is an important review. This movement from 3rd to 5th dimension is your journey of a lifetime. This is a trip that everyone on the planet is going to take with you. No one has a choice. Some may travel faster and more comfortably than others. Just as if you traveled by plane in first class accommodations your trip from New York to Los Angeles would be far more pleasant and faster than someone traveling by bus. But the bus trip would be far easier and more pleasant than someone traveling by riding lawn mower.

Everyone will take this trip! Each person will decide, consciously or subconsciously or by default their mode of transportation. Both the speed and enjoyment of their journey are products of individual choice.

Again, third-dimensional consciousness is defined by our five physical senses. If it can be tasted, smelled, felt, heard, seen, then we acknowledge it as real. Our reality is defined by those five senses. We talk about separation because I can feel where one thing starts and stops. For instance, my sense of touch tells me where the TV starts and I can feel where the TV stops. I can feel where the table starts. I can feel a book on a shelf, I know the separation from the book and the shelf. I know where one begins and the other ends. That separation is what defines the third dimension. It is that separation that creates our sense of duality. I am different than you. Good is different than bad. For everything, there is another thing that opposes it. The right has wrong and up has down. Almost everything has a duality or opposite involved.

In fifth dimensional consciousness, we stop seeing differences as defined by our five senses and instead see the oneness as defined by our heart. Fifth-dimensional consciousness is defined by that recognition that we are all one, and in that oneness, we are all part of the whole. Recognizing our oneness with the whole allows us to claim our greater nature. It allows us to be more light, to be more accepting, to be more honoring, to be more in peace, to be more in harmony. It's really what we all want in our lives. It doesn't matter how you label or define the whole, you just know that you are a part of it. The whole can be known as God, Great Spirit, Ala, the

Universe, Light, the Force, or Love. That part doesn't matter because we are all one and there can only be one.

The fourth dimension represents the space between third and fifth. The fourth dimension is the search state, it is the necessary space between NY and LA. It's what happens between third and fifth. If you tell someone about your travel plans, you talk about the destination; the places you travel through to get to your destination are usually not mentioned.

If you're reading this book you are in the fourth dimension. In the fourth dimension, you know there is something else so you are looking for it. You may at times be drawn back to the third dimension with some Earthly issues and at other times you may have flashes of fifth-dimensional insights. It is as if you are stretched out between 3rd and 5th dimension. One arm is in the third dimension and one arm is in the fifth dimension and you are being pulled back and forth between the two. One life experience will take you into the third dimension where you feel dense and troubled and then you will have a flash of fifth-dimensional love where you feel light, love, and so peaceful. This transition between 3rd and 5th is what the fourth dimension is. It can extremely difficult, but eventually, you will spend less time in 3rd until you move permanently into the oneness reality.

In third dimension you have a set of rules you must live by. In the fifth dimension, you have another set of rules you live by. In the fourth dimension, there are no rules. Indeed, you must willingly release the third-dimensional rules and choose to embrace fifth-dimensional rules.

In this chapter I will focus on the changes you will experience in your body, mind and spirit and what's holding you back. My goal is to help you recognize and release the things that keep you tied to the third dimension. This will make it much easier to join the fifth-dimensional party. I want you to see and celebrate your transformation. Imagine yourself recognizing, jumping with joy and saying, "Ahhh, I've arrived! Yeah for me! I'm harmonious. I'm loving. Nothing can take me out of my peaceful state." I will be there to celebrate with you!

Your life will be much more fun and glorious. So let's get busy and release your major anchors that keep pulling you back to the third dimension.

The Mind

You are not your mind. You have a mind. The mind has its own consciousness. Your life is best when you work in harmony with your mind. To do this you must gain mastery over your mind. I write about this in my book, ***Perfect Power in Consciousness: Seeking Truth through the Subconscious and Superconscious Mind*** and my future book, ***Mind Mastery***

The old mind has been set to keep you in a third-dimensional reality. It has been programmed to limit your world by processing everything through your five senses. It's one of the reasons that many of you are having mental issues (and I mean that in the most loving way). The old mind must let go of its comfortable safe known reality. It does not want to give up its place of power or its place of comfort.

As I tell you some of the major mind symptoms of letting go of 3rd dimension, you may say, "This is progress?" You may even join the mind in blocking the move to the 5th dimension. But trust me, it is progress.

Poor Memory & Forgetful Mind

It will become more difficult to remember things. Your memories will fade faster. This forgetting is not related to your age, or the medication you're on, or your family genetics. Flocking to get the right vitamins or supplements will not help. It is part of the process of moving from old mind to new mind; moving from the third dimension to the fifth dimension.

I am sure you have read or heard about the importance of "living in the now" or "being fully present in the moment." The mind blocks this with memories of the past or thoughts of the future. In order to be fully in the now, you are being asked to let go of your past and future. The universe is helping you live in the now by elimination your past. It's still there. You just won't remember it.

You will still have access to everything you need but you will get the info differently. Think about how we store information. Only a few decades ago, important information was written on paper and filed in file folders and placed in big bulky file cabinets that we could access at will. Move forward through time and now everything important is stored electronically. Even if you go to your doctor, no longer does he access a paper file, instead, his office opens up your electronic file and all the info is available to him or her. Same information but accessed differently.

When we type in the correct questions we will get the information we need. Think if it as "Googlizing your mind." No longer will we keep memories in our conscious mind. Instead, everything immediately goes to our subconscious and stored there until you make a request. Then that info is brought forward into your conscious mind on demand.

Lack of concentration

At one point in time in the American Education system, it was considered "bad" for a child to turn their head from side to side. Children were forced to stare ahead at the lesson and not "waste time" moving their head and attention to other things. They sat in rows always facing forward.

This may forward facing behavior may seem silly and hard to believe that this was actually an acceptable classroom practice, but it was. And in some ways, this is how your mind controls your attention. Imagine your old mind being that stern teacher forcing you to "face forward" or concentrate on a specific task before you.

But as you move into the fifth dimension, the old mind is forced to relinquish control. As this new mind takes over you will experience must more mental randomness. Because it is new for you to be taking in so much data, it may seem distracting. Old forms of concentration and focus will be more difficult to achieve. For some people, this will be unpleasant and even uncomfortable. You may even label this behavior as ADD (Attention Deficit Disorder) and reach for a pill to take you back to old familiar ways of concentrating. They may even help for the moment. But a pill won't stop progress.

As your new mind scans your world, you will be taking in endless data. It may even seem exhausting at first. It may be hard to process so much information flooding into your awareness from so many directions. Keep in mind the old mind has always done this but without your awareness. The less you try to attach to the information, the easier your life will become.

It is said that Einstein refused to learn his phone number because he could look it up. Apparently, he didn't learn anything that he could look up. So now become an Einstein. Don't attempt to hold on to everything. Just let it float over you. Being mindful is different than concentration.

That's right...in the place of "concentration" you will experience "mindfulness." It will carry all the same benefits with none of the limitation. Being fully present in every experience will serve you well.

Recently, I drove from Chicago to LA and back with my spiritually-gifted daughter. When she driving she kept three different navigation systems both voice and visually active. At different times, each device was promoting a different route and voicing different turns. For me it was confusing and I begged her turn off one or more of the systems. But she was in perfect comfort taking in the data from all three while deciding which to follow in that moment. She was fully attending, listening, and evaluating them without a flicker of confusion. That is a perfect example of the new 5D mind in action.

The less you struggle against the departure of your old 3D mind, the easier the transition to your new mind will be. Think of it as upgrading your computer. Have you ever upgraded an operating system? At first, it may seem awkward and unfamiliar. You may even wish you had the old system back, but then as you become more familiar with the new system, you recognize the benefits until eventually, you are glad you made the switch.

Your mind is being upgraded. You are moving from old Mind 3D to new Mind 5D. I promise you, you will love it once you become a bit more familiar with it!

Feeling Dizzy and/or Disorientation

Have you ever had a dream and you wake up with that dream still in your awareness? The dream can feel so real. You may even ask yourself, "Was it real?" As you orient yourself to your awaken state you may wonder, "Where am I? What's going on?" You have to re-orientate yourself to the physical state the "real world", (I know you can't see me, but I am using air quotes around the word "real". To explain that would require another book). At any rate, there is a period of reorientation when you move from your sleep state to your awake state. When you're flipping from third to the fifth dimension you also get those moments of disorientation. Those quick thoughts of "What's going on now? I'm not sure," because your thoughts, perceptions, and vibrations are actually changing, your belief systems are also changing. Your mental processes are changing and it makes you feel that, "What's happening here?" You can turn a corner and all of a sudden it's like, "Where am I? What's going on?" It's in that flash that you feel like, "Okay, I've got to get grounded in reality." Sometimes it comes with dizziness and the other kinds of things too.

Grounding yourself and staying grounded will help eliminate some of these feelings. There are lots of easy and quick ways to ground yourself: looking, smelling, touching plants; a quick 30-second meditation, reflection, or pause; deep slow breathes; a visualization of seeing yourself rooted to the earth; or setting the intention to go to your center or your happy place. There are zillions of ways to ground yourself. Ask and you will be told, Google and you will have millions of choices!

Life in a linear model

One of the functions of the old 3D mind was to keep us in a linear life. Both space and time unfolded in a predictable linear way. We could travel from here to there and our life had a past present and future. In the third dimension, we talk about things in a linear fashion. It was safe and easy.

If I wanted to *astral project*, or send my consciousness out into the world someplace, I operated in a linear model. I was separate from that projection of my consciousness. The US government spent millions of dollars teaching people how to do astral projection to create better spies. It's very real and it's very possible. It's also very third dimensional.

When you're in the fifth dimension you no longer feel the need to send out a projection of your consciousness. Instead, you expand your consciousness. In a fully grounded 5D world you are not limited to a linear life. I love the movie ***Bill and Ted's Excellent Adventure*** because it captured the essence of time in a non-linear form. More recently the movie, ***Arrival*** made the truth of non-linear time a bit clearer. I recommend both movies. Gather a few like-minded friends, and a bowl of popcorn. You will want to spend some time reflecting on what you just watched after each movie.

In a 5D world, your mind will support your expansion in so many ways. Ways that you can't now imagine. A well-grounded advanced 5D mind will also allow you to expand your consciousness, create multiple experiences that are all feeding into your awareness. I see it more as a circular model and it is very different and a very cool process.

Brain Fog
You just have to turn on PBS to see some special on brain fog, and losing our memory. All of those things are part of this evolved consciousness. It's not a bad thing. You don't need a special herbal supplement, you don't need to do mental exercises, although they can't hurt you. Brain fog, literally clouding and releasing of this focus is part of this evolution into a fifth-dimensional consciousness where the mind no longer controls or reigns supreme. It becomes a tool which you turn on when you need it, and otherwise, it's at rest. Just like your car, if you need to take a trip you go and get in the car,

and you turn it on, and you use it. When you're done with your trip you turn the car off and it's at a state of rest. That is the perfect analogy for fifth-dimensional consciousness and how the mind works. The mind is a creator. You turn it on when you want to create or manifest.

Benefits of a Fifth Dimensional Mind:

Now it is time to look at the blessings that are hiding in the brain fog...and there are many. Here are some of my favorites.

No limits.

Since you have no limits you will be amazed at what you can accomplish. Productivity and accomplishments will soar but not in the old ways. New definitions will emerge.

Research has been conducted with hundreds of people in a ballroom. They were asked to mix and mingle. Later they were asked what they could remember. Most people could recall their conversations. They were even aware when they heard someone mention their name. But under hypnosis, these same people could recount *all* the conversations going on in the room and were not limited to only those they were engaged in. The 3D mind was consciously aware of their conversations but the 5D mind heard and stored them all. This study scientifically demonstrated that we are always taking in everything. Now, with fifth-dimensional consciousness, you can take in everything and be able to access everything.

The unlimited 5D mind will allow you to be listening to someone, be fully aware of everything that is going on around you, and be outside the experience consciously aware of your reaction to the experience, etc. It gets very convoluted and very big. That's a good thing, except you will feel, "I can't concentrate anymore, I'm so distracted." Remember this is progress, stop holding yourself back by judging it.

Think of it as blinders being removed. I loved being in the south and spending lots of time on working farms. They would put blinders on work horses to limit their sight. They didn't get spooked or distracted by what they couldn't see. The 3D mind is like blinders on humanity. They were there to protect us and to keep us focused. Now, the blinders are being removed and you are being forced to deal with the many distractions of life. Your 5D mind operates on lots of channels and is perfectly conscious of all of them simultaneously.

Recently, I had an experience where in the old third-dimensional mind would have been impossible. My ability to focus and concentrate would have stopped it. I would have had to block out all the distractions.

I didn't do it intentionally; I was simply doing what came naturally to me at the time. Until…I realized what I was doing.

I had two online classes that I wanted to take that were occurring at the same time. One was four hours webinar and one was eight hours. I couldn't decide which I wanted to listen to and which I wanted to skip, so I didn't. I decided to take them both. I set up two different computers and I watched both classes simultaneously. I really didn't even notice I was doing it at first. I was able to pay perfect attention to both of them. I didn't switch my attention back and forth. I literally watched both in real time and took notes of them both. In fact, I had two different notepads. One pad per class and I took great notes for both of them. Because my mind gets super active when I am learning new stuff, I also had a deck of 3x5 cards on my lap because as these two classes triggered action steps for me. Those action steps were recorded on a card as well. Over the four hours, I filled two notepads and close to a hundred follow-up cards. I was doing three things simultaneously without losing a beat.

When I realized what I was doing I took pictures because it was amazed at the ease of my actions. I was able to perfectly attend two completely different presentations simultaneously, as well as record my thoughts and follow up actions. At first, it wasn't even unusual until I observed myself doing all this. Then I was amazed at my wondrous new mind ability.

That's the new fifth-dimensional mind in action. It is not limited. It loosens its grip, it no longer controls or limits our experience, but we're able to do anything and everything that we choose to do.

Intentional Manifestations

Your mind is both a creation and a creator. The mind creates our world. The old 3D mind was creating nonstop. It created every thought we had and thus created chaos in our life. Movies like the *Secret* and countless books have attempted to show how we are creator beings. But at the 3D level, we exerted little control over our minds endless creations.

In the third dimension, you see the manifest as a linear process. I have a thought, I have a dream, I have a vision, I have a want. I send it out into the universe, and then it's created and then sent back to me. It operates in a linear model. In the fourth dimension, you are in transition. The fourth dimension is the exploration. It's the place that you're beginning to formulate tools and techniques to live comfortably in the fifth dimension. In the fifth dimension, when you want to manifest you understand that you must simply align with that energy. There's not a set time frame, there's not a specific and structured sequence of events. Both of those are 3D. Manifesting in 5D is intentional. It's about creating in that oneness of all that is. You center in the energy with total trust. You align yourself with the creative force. Not seriously, not routinely but with joy. You play and realize that whatever it is that we're aligning with already exists in the universe, and that's a whole other place.

Learning to still the mind has been a major lesson on our journey from third to the fifth dimension. A still mind doesn't create randomly. As we learn to control and operate our mind responsibility we will gain the ability to manifest intentionally. This is such a big topic that it will have its own book soon. For now, I will just plant the seed…you must learn to still your mind. Until you do your old 3D mind will continue to run amuck.

For most of us, the old 3D mind has operated with little guidance or support from you, but as you learn to work in harmony with your mind, this will change. Read my book, ***Perfect Power in Consciousness*** for directions on how to do this.

In the fifth dimension when we're truly living in the recognition that everything in your life and everyone in your life is your creation. You are solely responsible for every aspect of your existence. When you are living in that truth you also know that everybody else is living in their truth and their life circumstances are a product of their creation. If there is a bump in their road then you know that's part of their journey. You don't have to go, "Oh, poor them." You go, "Wow, that was a learning lesson. I wonder what they will learn from that?" Compassion changes totally in the process. You no longer go, "Oh, poor thing." You go, "Yep, that's a bump. What did you learn from that?" Sympathy changes to compassion and empathy. Enabling ends and responsibility is the law. In that fifth-dimensional consciousness, you are responsible for everything in your world and you recognize that everybody else is equally responsible. No longer are pity parties allowed.

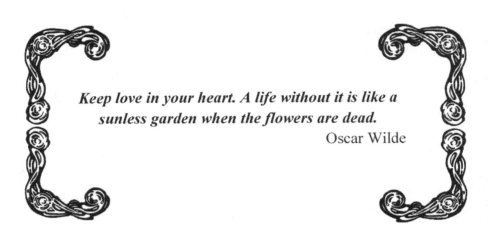

Keep love in your heart. A life without it is like a sunless garden when the flowers are dead.

Oscar Wilde

~14~

The Body and the Necessary Changes

"To keep the body in good health is a duty... otherwise we shall not be able to keep our mind strong and clear."

Buddha

Your physical body is a magnificent gift and it is the reason we chose to be born. The physical body is a perfect creation you designed to assist you with your lessons here on Earth.

You are not your body. You have a body. Your body has a consciousness separate from you. Your body is the truth teller, while your mind is a trickster. The body tells you truth whereas your mind feeds you stories. Learning to listen to your body is incredibly important.

Your body is the same body you have had throughout all your life experiences, past present and future (remember no linear model exists, it was simply a product of your 3D mind). The body holds all your unresolved emotional issues). If you are a hoarder of physical stuff, more than likely you also hold on to emotional stuff. The issue of letting go is what you must deal with.

If you hold on to your grievances, hurts, and other emotional issues, chances are pretty great that you also have weight issues. The added weight helps the body support your unresolved emotional issues. Start dealing with them and there is an excellent chance you will lose your unwanted pounds.

Your body also carries your vibrational frequency which also determines your dimensional state. A 3D person vibrates slower than a 4D or 5D person. You can't move into 5D until you have dealt with the emotional issues that are keeping you anchored to 3D.

Unresolved emotional issues are stored in the body, creating spots of disharmony. Long term disharmony creates dis-ease in the body. Dis-ease creates disease. Two excellent books I would recommend on this topic are Louis Hays', ***You Can Heal Your Body***, and Deb Shapiro's, ***Your Body Speaks***.

As your body attempts to raise its vibration for its ascent into the fifth dimension, it begs you to deal with old issues, some from this lifetime and some from others. Face them and deal because they won't go away until you let go of them. For a hoarder, cleaning out the basement and throwing out the garbage is hard. Eventually, they must either decide to throw out the trash or live in it. Emotionally that is what every human on this planet is facing. What's your emotional issue? Fear, anger, hurt, separation, doubt, worry, concern or other emotional wounds are crying out to be healed. So deal! Clean up your emotional basement. Just because they can't be seen, they are still impacting the quality of your life.

Be Kind to your body
Your body is a great gift and should be treated as your best friend. You can't get there from here without total and complete cooperation of your body. Consider your body as your traveling

companion on this junket through life. The better you treat it, the happier it will be, and the more enjoyable will be your journey.

This was a lesson I had to learn the hard way. I treated my body like an old junk car. I gave it as much attention as required for survival and not one ounce more. I feed it (but not very well), no exercise, and little pleasure. I was proud of my workaholic lifestyle. Productivity was my king.

I have been guided to love and care for my body—and I really meant to do better when I had time. I was told to take time off and play more…and I really meant to. Then bam, I had a car accident which put me in the hospital and physical therapy.

This experience taught me any things…and I know for sure we are not our body. Your body was created and chosen as your vehicle through this life experience. It has a separate consciousness and set of needs. As you learn to listen to your body, you will know what these needs are. Since each body is different, the path to restore our body will be different for everyone.

Your body is designed to be your greatest friend, and teacher. It is the shape and form you have created to serve your purposes in this life and it is a composite of all the bodies you have occupied throughout your physical existence. It is charged with the responsibility of carrying forward and storing all your unresolved emotional issues until you are strong enough and brave enough to face them.

Depending on how you treat your body, it can be your best friend or your worst enemy. Many of your most profound lessons come through the body experience. Your body must carry the physical vibration of your spirit. You can only achieve a certain level of spiritual ascension without expanding and purifying your cellular body.

NEVER, never take your body for granted. It holds the key to your success or failure of your spiritual mission in this physical world. Your body *is* the sacred temple of your divine spirit. Meeting its needs will allow you to achieve your greatest dreams and loftiest goals. Love your body unconditionally—no matter what!

Drink Lots of Water

Your body's main ingredient is water. Scientists suggest you must drink eight glasses (eight ounces) each day just to flush out your physical system to maintain health. But for spiritual ascension and physical purification, you may need much more than this.

Your body will only release the same amount of liquid as you drink. Therefore, if you drink only two glasses of water per day, then only one-fourth of your body fluids are cleaned. The other three-fourths are the old, stale, impure liquids that are filled with discarded impurities (This is an unpleasant thought, isn't it?).

It is important that the water is clear water (as opposed to tea, coffee, juice, or flavored water) since any flavored water must be filtered through your body as a food and does not have the same cleansing abilities.

Consequently, drinking water is important just to maintain your health, but as you go through the frequency acceleration process you will need even more water. I found that I would often drink up to a gallon or more per day. If you can imagine this process as being like changing the oil in your car, you will begin to see how important the water truly is. Now there is great debate over bottled or tap water. Unfortunately, I can't provide you with the *right* answer because there isn't one. In the end, there is just a choice.

According to my spiritual sources when water is taken out of circulation, as it is when it is bottled, the living life force contained in the water dies and is not as good for the body even though it may be purer. On the other hand, tap water often contains unhealthy levels of chemicals and heavy metals. So, in the end, you must decide the best choice for you. I choose to filter my tap water. Regardless of your choice, water is always better for you if it is blessed as this greatly increases the frequency of the water.

Best to use love infused blessed water as it carries the highest vibration.

There are several techniques for infusing love and blessing your water. All of them are very easy and costs nothing. (1) You can send the water light and love. This can be done by seeing it as in a vision, saying it or just trusting that your thoughts have created this as your reality. (2) You can say, "I bless this water" (out loud or silently). (3) You can ask God and/or the angels to bless the water or fill it with love. Any of these techniques are equally effective.

In fact, if you would like to test the effectiveness of these techniques, here is a simple taste test. First, take a drink of water. Really taste it and see how it feels in your mouth. Next, use one of the above techniques to raise the frequency of the water. Now taste it again. Can you tell a difference? Most people can. Some say it is sweeter, clearer or even seems softer in their mouth. You have actually changed the molecular makeup of the water.

If you feel really scientific, you can also do this to food. Take two dishes of food, fill one with love and then let them both rot. They will rot differently. The blessed food will last longer than the unblessed dish. It is a fun activity for children! They love to watch food spoil and it is a wonderful demonstration of the power of love.

Water is the life force of Mother Earth. As your physical frequency accelerates so must your intake of water. Water allows each cell to feel the frequency more clearly by increasing its resonance. Water helps the cells of your body hold an ever-increasing higher molecular frequency, as it helps to flush away the old cells. This flushing is necessary because each cell has an individual frequency range, with its predetermined high and low. In order for the cell to extend this range, old cells must be constantly replaced with new ones. The new cells are then able to extend ever higher with their frequency. Water helps to flush out the system, washing away these old slower vibratory cells.

If you want to experience the ultimate in super empowered water, then you might want to experience the power of a real *mineral water*. It is easy to make and carries a very high vibration, which your body will respond to very quickly. Take a clean rose quartz, amethyst, or clear quartz crystal and place it in a jug of blessed water. Place the water containing the crystal in the sun for a minimum of 20 minutes. Drink it sparingly, perhaps a few glasses per day. This treatment really accelerates the body's frequency, so be prepared for the side effects.

There are books available on making gem elixirs as this homemade mineral water is called. But if you stick to these three stones I suggest you won't get yourself in any trouble. I do suggest you buy one before you begin experimenting with your own varieties of mineral water, as some stones can be toxic. The three stones I mentioned are always safe to play with. The rose quartz accelerates the love frequency, the amethyst is a sonic purifier and the quartz crystal amplifies and empowers. If you drink too much mineral water it will have the same type effect as drinking lots of caffeine, you will get extremely wired. Some people even experience accelerated diarrhea.

Eat Whole and Healthy Food

"You are what you eat" is a spiritual truth. Vibrationally, what you put in your body in any form impacts your body. In choosing your food, it is best to consult with your body and not some expert or author. Your body is your best advisor as to your diet. My body prefers organic and fresh, yours may want something different. Let common sense and your internal body wisdom guide you.

If you allow the process, your diet will be adjusted to bring in the elements needed, as well as eliminate those that do not serve the physical you. Your diet may change frequently and quickly, so don't stock up on a favorite food. For two weeks I dined almost exclusively on avocado and sprout sandwiches. I wanted nothing else, this craving stopped as suddenly as it started and I was left with a refrigerator full of sprouts.

I find the vibration of the food is all-important. I can now tell by the way my body feels when I eat a carrot with an attitude or an unhappy cucumber. I intentionally select happy and contented food and my body is grateful. Trust your inner guidance or in this case, trust your gut!

Regardless of the food you purchase, blessing it prior to eating it really helps the process.

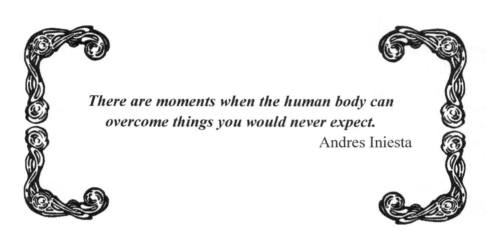

There are moments when the human body can overcome things you would never expect.

Andres Iniesta

~15~

Action Steps for Ascension: How to speed up your movement into 5th Dimension

"The historic ascent of humanity, taken as a whole, may be summarized as a succession of victories of consciousness over blind forces - in nature, in society, in man himself."

Leon Trotsky

Surrender. Follow your heart.

It sounds so easy because it is. Stop resisting!

Imagine you have a team of top coaches guiding through this journey from 3D to 5D. They are helping you find successfully guide you along your path. As long as you call on truth using the truth mantra, you cannot be misled.

Trust.

I love beaches. When I go to my center, I imagine it to be a beautiful beach. When I am feeling troubled or confused, I go to my beach. I call this my happy place. I always get what I need in my happy place.

Find your happy place.

Your center and your happy place are the same place. It is the state of where you are most aligned with the universal energies. It is where you are most aligned with your higher self, with your spiritual guidance. It's a very powerful place for you and I'd like you to set the intention to do it now. As soon as you've set the intention, you are there. No magic, no deep breathing, no hypnosis, just be in that trust and move to your happy place.

What I'd like to do, because we're moving into a vibrational world, is we're going to allow a spiritual guide to be there with you to make sure that everything you need and want to experience will happen in divine, perfect order. We want to make sure that you travel safely. We want to make sure that you're always protected and you always feel that protection because if you get into worry and doubt, you can be pulled back into that creation. You don't want your old past creation, you want you to surrender to the new possibilities.

The ascension of consciousness is the process of allowing. The awakening empowers humanity to become intentional creators of their individual and collective reality and destiny.

The ascension is also a process of vibrational change. Moving from a slower and lower third-dimensional rate to a higher and faster fifth-dimensional rate. It is this vibrational shift that will support the Earth's healing and transformation. These shifts don't and can't happen in one action or one moment of time, but it is a continual increase as a result of the accumulation of your collective intentions, thoughts, words, and actions. Every thought no matter how insignificant it feels will either increase or decrease your vibrational rate.

The following suggestions are given to help you to awaken to your true self and to your Divine mission. I trust these suggestions will be helpful. Read them with an open heart and feel your own cellular evolution.

Teach these to your children. Demonstrate them in your life. Model them for your friends.

The directions for ascension are clear and can be used by all people of all ages. These steps will enable you to achieve its greatest good.

Talk to the Heavenly God Source

Remember, you are not now nor never have been alone. Your heavenly creator is always available for counsel. This is not an outside entity sitting on a throne in a place called Heaven, but a loving presence that is a part of everything and everyone.

Take time to talk to the God Source, for all is heard. This can be accomplished in the form of conversation as you drive or go about your daily routine or through a more formal prayer. The choice matters not, for either way you are recognizing and acknowledging this Infinite Intelligence presence in your life. You are awakening that vibration in your life. You are bridging the Divine frequency with your thoughts. This will have a positive effect on your own vibrational frequency and your life. With each communication, either formal or informal, the relationship is strengthened.

Ask for Help
In your conversations with God, ask for what you want. Remember that God, or any of the Divine servants, can do nothing *unless you request help*. Free will is the Divine law. No one is allowed to intervene without a request. Ask for help, ask to be shown the way, ask for clarification of your purpose, ask for *"this or something better, for my highest and best good and the highest and best good of all concerned."* By using this phrase when you ask for something,

you are recognizing that there is a higher view than your Earthly eyes allow. You are giving those who have a better vantage point an opportunity to work on your behalf. You are allowing the God Essence and the heavenly guardians to assist you while you are in the physical.

Be clear with the end product but do not try to dictate the process to be used to get there. For instance, ask for the help in getting the book written, but don't dictate the form the help will take. Solutions beyond your wildest imagination will become evident. Just be very clear about what you need and why you need it.

When the time comes that you feel you are ready to surrender personal will to Divine will, know that you must surrender 100% to really be of use. When you do this you become like a professional dancer. You become a willing and capable dance partner, able to follow the subtle guidance from the divine. You are not a puppet, but an important partner in the process. You bring your skills and abilities to the table, not an empty vessel.

God needs to work through many helpers on beloved Mother Earth to achieve the desired end. Each willing partner becomes the right hand of God, allowing this Goodness to work through you. This is the way to anchor heaven to Earth.

Reciting the Lord's Prayer with Divine intent assists with this process.

Give Thanks
Gratitude is a great vibrational accelerator! Give thanks for receiving the answers to your prayers, as you pray for them. This is a demonstration of faith and will help your prayers to be answered. Do not doubt the outcome. Prayers are always answered. An attitude of gratitude assists you in the opening to a greater world of abundance. *Know that whatever comes into your life is for your best and highest good.* Be appreciative for everything.

Always look for the good and the needed lesson in every situation, no matter what it looks like or how painful the experience. Trust that you will appreciate these lessons later, so instead of waiting to appreciate them now.

Take Time to Listen

Take time to listen to the wee, small voice. Learn to recognize this source of wisdom even under the most chaotic of circumstances. This process can be as simple as lying in the bathtub, clearing your mind, and allowing your consciousness to float along. Or it can come as the result of a more formal meditation with structure and rules. The point is to become intentionally receptive to the thoughts and voice of God in your daily life. Be receptive to thoughts that float into your conscious awareness. Learn to differentiate between your own mental ramblings and a divine inspiration.

For many people *meditation* is used to teach a more formal and disciplined form of *listening* is used to develop this connection. Since there are many forms of meditation being taught, the process used does not matter. Anything that permits you to still your mind for at least three minutes will serve this purpose.

During this listening time, have no expectations. Listen to your heart, soul, and inner guidance. You may gradually feel the need for longer periods of silence. The length of time is secondary to the ability to listen from the heart and recognize the difference between the mental and spiritual source of the thoughts. Taking time to listen creates a space for your connection to the divine to strengthen and develop.

Do not become concerned because you have friends that see vivid images during their meditations and you see nothing. Remember that each person has different needs and has developed different skills over many lifetimes. Trust that you have what you need and they have what they need.

Don't become concerned if you drift off to sleep during times of stillness. It may be that your conscious mind feels you are not ready for conscious awareness, thus it blocks your awareness. It cannot, however, block the experience. So keep on keeping on. Eventually, you will convenience your conscious mind that you are ready for full awareness.

As you learn to live in a state of internal harmony, your mind will gain confidence and surrender control to your soul/spirit. These mental blocks are cosmic safety features and are precautions taken to ensure you are protected from self-destruction and internal torture.

If your quiet time allows you to feel less stressed and more at peace within yourself, the meditation has served its intended purpose. Trust that this listening time what is happening is in your best interest and be grateful.

Still the Conscious Mind
This is related to the act of meditation but different. Learning to listen, including meditation, is an intentional act at a specific time. Whereas learning to still your mind, is an on-going process that is vital to your reconnecting to the divine. The condition of your mind will affect your life every minute of your day.

It is true that in mediation you are learning how to still the mind, but that stillness must continue 24/7. Stilling the mind is like learning to turn down the volume of your radio that distracts you from fully focusing your attention on your present moment.

Have you ever gone to the theater and sat in front of a couple who engage in conversation through the entire show? Then, you know how distracting it can be. After a while, you want to turn around and tell them to be quiet so you can enjoy the performance.

A mind out of control is like always being in the presence of a verbal distraction. You may be talking to a friend and the mind chatters, "Look at that! Do you believe that hair? Boy, she looks old... Wonder if she's back with her husband..." In this example, the rambling mind separates you from your experience.

Pay special attention to your own mind the next time you go to the theater. If your mind is out of control, you may notice your runaway mind. As you are trying to enjoy the movie, it may chatter (just like the couple chatting behind you), "That actress could do a better job... Did you see that?... Wasn't that fake-looking?... That was dangerous..." If you have an on-going dialogue with yourself in this situation, then chances are pretty good that you have an ongoing conversation with yourself in all life situations. If it was someone sitting next to you (instead of inside your head), after a while you wouldn't hesitate to tell them to be quiet. Treat your mind the same way and recognize how annoying your mind can be as well. Don't allow your mind to ramble without limits. Just because you have grown accustomed to it, doesn't make it right or healthy.

Yes, it is possible to still the mind. Use the steps listed above.

You will feel the difference almost immediately. You will be able to experience life and people without all the distractions. You will be more fully present for your life. By bringing your mind into harmony, you will find that it will become more available to assist when needed but not so invasive in your experiences.

If you have difficulty stilling the mind, talk to it lovingly but firmly, as a loving parent would talk to a disobedient five-year-old child. Tell it why it is important for it to be still and why this is in the best interests of all. If this does not work for you, ask the angels for help.

The mind has been given the job of guardian to the gates of knowing. This powerful position determines what is known and not known at the conscious level. This power can be intoxicating and hard for the mind to relinquish. The mind may not readily and willingly give up this powerful position. "You," and not your mind, have free will and the right to choose, so persist, if it is for your highest good. Remember "you" are not your mind, your mind works for you. "You," the spiritual soul part of you, must gain dominion over your mind to achieve the divine reconnection you desire.

Once you learn to still your mind, you will become much more receptive to inner guidance and be able to recognize this divine intuition in every moment. This is the reward and purpose of learning to still the mind.

Follow Your Inner Guidance

After learning to hear divine guidance, the next step is gaining confidence in it. Once confidence is gained, then you must *follow your inner guidance* and *trust this divine intuition.* Begin by asking for the ability to discern the difference between your mind and inner guidance in your everyday life. Allow truth to enter your consciousness. As you get this divine guidance, take action. *Do the thing that you know to do.* You must take action if action is called for or requested.

In the beginning, this inner guidance will not be earth shaking. Rest if you feel the need to rest. Eat, sleep, work, and play based on the dictates of your inner voice, not by established routines or the desires of others. As you make a commitment to the Divine to cooperate with the divine will be receptive to directions. If your heart is sincere, the directions will come. Then, your level of trust will help you to follow the directions given.

There is a story I found on the internet that illustrates this well...

A young man had been to Wednesday night Bible Study. The Pastor had shared about listening to God and obeying the Lord's voice. The young man couldn't help but wonder, "Does God still speak to people?" After service, he went out with some friends for coffee and pie and they discussed the message. Several different ones talked about how God had led them in different ways. It was about ten o'clock when the young man started driving home. Sitting in his car, he just began to pray, "God...If you still speak to people speak to me. I will listen. I will do my best to obey."

As he drove down the main street of his town, he had the strangest thought to stop and buy a gallon of milk. He shook his head and said out loud, "God is that you?" He didn't get a reply and started on toward home.

But again, the thought, buy a gallon of milk. The young man thought about Samuel and how he didn't recognize the voice of God, and how little Samuel ran to Eli. "Okay, God, in case that is you, I will buy the milk."

It didn't seem like too hard a test of obedience. He could always use the milk. He stopped and purchased the gallon of milk and started off toward home. As he passed Seventh Street, he again felt the urge, "Turn Down that street."

This is crazy he thought and drove on past the intersection. Again, he felt that he should turn down Seventh Street. At the next intersection, he turned back and headed down Seventh. Half jokingly, he said out loud, "Okay, God, I will". He drove several blocks when suddenly, he felt like he should stop.

He pulled over to the curb and looked around. He was in semi-commercial area of town. It wasn't the best but it wasn't the worst of neighborhoods either. The businesses were closed and most of the houses looked dark like the people were already in bed. Again, he sensed something, "Go and give the milk to the people in the house across the street."

The young man looked at the house. It was dark and it looked like the people were either gone or they were already asleep. He started to open the door and then sat back in the car seat. "Lord, this is insane. Those people are asleep and if I wake them up, they are going to be mad and I will look stupid." Again, he felt like he should go and give the milk.

Finally, he opened the door, "Okay God, if this is you, I will go to the door and I will give them the milk. If you want me to look like a crazy person, okay. I want to be obedient. I guess that will count for something but if they don't answer right away, I am out of here."

He walked across the street and rang the bell.

He could hear some noise inside. A man's voice yelled out, "Who is it? What do you want?" Then the door opened before the young man could get away.

The man was standing there in his jeans and T-shirt. He looked like he just got out of bed. He had a strange look on his face and he didn't seem too happy to have some stranger standing on his doorstep. "What is it?"

The young man thrust out the gallon of milk, "Here, I brought this to you." The man took the milk and rushed down a hallway. Then from down the hall came a woman carrying the milk toward the kitchen. The man was following her holding a baby. The baby was crying. The man had tears streaming down his face. The man began speaking and half crying, "We were just praying. We had some big bills this month and we ran out of money. We didn't have any milk for our baby. I was just praying and asking God to show me how to get some milk."

His wife in the kitchen yelled out, "I ask him to send an Angel with some. Are you an Angel?"

The young man reached into his wallet and pulled out all the money he had on him and put in the man's hand. He turned and walked back toward his car and the tears were streaming down his face. He knew that God still answers prayers.

This is a perfect example of how God speaks to you. My life has been filled with such experiences. I could literally fill a book.

But it is not the same for all people. For some, your inner guidance may be audible voices or clear vision, but for most, it is the gentle stirring of our soul. It is what I call that wee small voice. Learn to listen and follow. But be discerning, there are real mental health issues. If you are concerned...check it out.

The truth is that this Divine Source speaks to everyone but not everyone is listening. The divine whispers and insights divine inspiration in the moment. It is important to have a still mind and a willing spirit to act on these inspirations. The Divine is found in the spontaneity of action. The more you follow these divine inspiration the more empowered they become. Sometimes it's the simplest things that we are asked to do that have the greatest impact on us and the world. Your must prepare yourself to listen, trust, and act on these whisperings. It will bless both you and the world.

Learn to Exist in Your State of Center

Centering yourself is the intentional art of harmonizing the physical, mental and spiritual aspects of you so that you are at one with yourself and the universe. In the beginning, it requires intentional action and focused effort. It is only from this place of center that can you be fully "plugged in" to the divine. Being centered allows your spiritual nature to bring into alignment with your physical and mental energy for maximum benefit. It is the process of reconnecting the totality of who you are with the oneness of life.

Being centered can be compared to the difference in driving an automatic transmission or manual transmission car. When you are centered your gears are shifted automatically for you. It allows you to always be in the state if the perfect existence or using the car analogy to be operating in your appropriate "gear." But just as in the development of cars, we begin by being a manual transmission. We must be consciously aware and intentionally shift our own gears. It really is like driving a car with manual transmission and learning to shift gears. Over time, shifting into center becomes "automatic." After that, it no longer requires conscious effort.

Imagine driving your car in first gear all the time. Think how the engine would struggle to keep up the speed and it attempts to move faster. Think of the added wear on the transmission.

There is nothing wrong with first gear. It is appropriate for low speeds. But when you get up to 10-15 miles per hour, you had better know how to shift gears if you want to take care of your car. People who are accustomed to driving a manual transmission don't need to look at the speedometer; they know, through their familiarity with the sound and feel of the engine, when it is time to shift. They become attuned to it and respond to its unspoken needs. Your life is shifting from the 3D gear to 5D. It will run much smoother.

Each engine, like each person, is different. Each engine requires shifting at slightly different times. This requires each driver to listen to their engine and respond accordingly.

Most people have been running their engines at a relatively slow speed—a first gear of sorts, it may not feel like you have been going slow, but, in the cosmic sense, you have. Because of the speeding up of time and the other subtle Earth energy shifts, most people are now feeling the need to shift to a higher, more comfortable gear. Centering is the process of doing just that. The process of physically shifting gears is like the car engine that speeds up when the gears are shifted allowing the engine to run easier.

Being in your center allows you to do more, achieve more, while being in greater peace. The faster you go in your center (the higher your frequency), the more still you become, much like the gyroscope in the center of an ocean liner, which stabilizes it in the face of buffeting waves. In your center, you become immersed in the stillness and the internal place of peace. It is the only place where "the joy that passes understanding" can be found.

As you learn to intentionally center yourself, you begin to recognize the moment that you fall out of your center—like a car running in the wrong gear. This awareness allows you to quickly and easily move back to your place of center.

Next time you are feeling stressed, take a moment to focus your attention on how you are feeling physically. Pay attention to your heart, lungs, emotional well-being, and your mind. This will help you know what your body feels like when it needs centering. More than likely, even though you are used to this physical condition, you are racing your engine and it desperately needs to be shifted.

The process you use to center yourself is not important—the fact that you are intentionally putting your focus on centering is all important.

Any techniques you use will work. They are equally powerful, *for it is your intent that makes it happen.* There are "experts" that teach long, time-consuming and complicated strategies for centering. It doesn't have to be complicated to be effective. It doesn't have to be time-consuming to have a great impact on your life. All you need is clear intention and perfect trust that it can happen in the instant.

Chose a technique and do it. Thirty to forty-five seconds will do the trick. Feel your feelings now.

For an added boost, take another three deep and slow breaths. Each time focus on breathing in Divine will, universal harmony, and/or Christ light. You may use any image or word that you desire, for all of these things are the same source.

Consciously breathe out anything that does not serve you. After the three breaths, stop and again sense how you feel.

This is what you feel like when you are in Divine harmony. This is what it feels like to be centered. As you do this more often, you will begin to sense when you are out of center/connection/alignment; thus, you can learn to recognize when you need to shift your own gears.

Soon, the time will come when you are always in your place of center and Divine connection. The more you are in the center, the more uncomfortable it will be for you to be out of center.

Maintain Integrity in All You Do

Now is the time to maintain personal and professional integrity in everything you do. Integrity has been defined as having your belief and value structure in agreement with or in harmony with your behavior.

You must live your beliefs. Now is the time to walk your talk and talk your walk. It is the sacred 18-inch journey from head to heart. It is going from knowing truth (head) to living truth (heart).

Integrity requires you to align your intentions, thoughts, words, actions, and beliefs. Every outward thought, word, or action must be in harmony with your internal belief system. If they are not, then you must stand accountable for the differences.

If you say or believe you are an honest person, but freely alter the truth to fit your needs, you are out of integrity. If you know and admit to yourself that you say what needs to be said to fit your purpose, then you are in integrity.

If you feel angry toward someone and yet pretend to be loving toward them, you are out of integrity; whereas, if you recognize and honor your angry feelings and deal with them (which does not imply taking action toward the other person, but just being honest in your dealings with them), you are in integrity.

If you do not feel like giving someone a hug, yet do it anyway, you are out of integrity. If you do not feel like giving someone a hug and own and respect your feelings, you are in integrity.

If you say yes when you want to say no, you are out of integrity. If you go along with something you know is not right, you are out of integrity. If you confront it and/or refuse to be a part of it then, you are in integrity.

Integrity is a very important part of the new day on Earth. All people must move into integrity to carry the highest vibration. Integrity does not imply that you must be perfect or above reproach, but it does mean that you must be responsible for every thought, word, and deed and always be in harmony with your beliefs. The art of "talking out of both sides of your mouth" will no longer be acceptable.

Unconditionally Love
Unconditional love is unconditional acceptance. No judgment, no separation, and no resistance are allowed. Any of these takes you out of this universal unconditional love. Unconditional love requires you to go through life with your heart wide open—totally vulnerable and intimate with the world.

Maintaining this love vibration can be a challenge. Life seems to give us many reasons not to, so at first, it may be difficult. Do your best and ask for help. Gradually you will be able to stay in this unconditional love mode for longer and longer periods of time. When you fail to feel love when you feel your heart begin to shut down, investigate to find out why. These can be important lessons for your own growth.

Periodically stop and ask the angels, higher self, or friends from other dimensions to fill your totality with love. As you feel these wonderful sensations (for they *always* respond), give thanks and act in a way that maintains these feelings. This is somewhat like walking while balancing a book on your head. It is difficult at first because it causes you to concentrate on the act of walking. It becomes easier with practice.

You must allow the love essence to come through you at all times. *Your inner being is all love essence.* This heart open, unconditional love condition, allows your inner nature to seep through your outer physical shell.

Free Yourself from Anyone or Anything That Does Not Serve You

There are many forces: intentional and accidental, human and nonhuman, terrestrial and extraterrestrial, that may prevent you from moving into your highest frequency and into your place of power. Becoming aware of how you feel when these lower vibrational forces are influencing you is the first step in freeing yourself from their bondage.

Once again, once recognized as a limiting influence, a simple action is all that is required. A prayer, affirmation, or visualization can release you from their influence.

For example, an affirmation may be....

I am worthy and I deserve good just as I am. I am influenced by those things and people that further my growth and bring divine truth to my life. I attract that which is for my highest and best good and the highest and best good for all concerned.

For all times, I am released and protected from all that dims my light, slows my step, and/or the influence of anything or anyone that impedes my progress, or interferes with my life.

*I am surrounded by a shield of love which protects me and
transmutes all internal and external influences to its highest love
vibrational form. So be it! It is done!*

I find repeating an affirmation three times to be most effective.
Affirmation can also be spoken as a prayer. Repeat your
affirmations morning and evening until its truth is your truth. You
will feel how long it takes.

Help Others *Only* When Asked

This is a spiritual "mind your own business and keeps your effort
directed to your own path."

Helping others can often be a way to avoid dealing with your own
stuff, while it interferes with the life path of another. Assuming the
other person is over the age of 13 and fully capable, you must be
asked for help, only then can you help. You can *offer* your help if
you feel the impulse to do so, but never take action on their behalf—
even in your mind, unless they ask/tell you to do so.

Everyone on the planet is on a personal growth journey, and
although you may think you know what is best for them, but you
don't. If you take action without their permission, you assume the
karmic obligation for their experience. (I have on occasion been
guided to do something for another. I do follow my inner guidance
but I always give permission to the angels or their higher the right to
undo my actions.)

It is not your job to pray for their healing/recovery (unless asked), as
this assumes they are "broken" and needs to be fixed. Many of
humanity's greatest lessons have come from their challenging times.
Even Jesus, one of the greatest healers, didn't heal anyone unless
invited. Follow his model.

By the same token, beings of the highest realm are also honor bound by these same laws. They too may only help you if you ask. So learn to step up and ask for help (something not easy for many people). Do not hesitate to ask for what you want or need from both your physical and spiritual friends. You might be surprised at how many others are willing to lend a hand when you need it.

Trust

Trust. Trust. Trust!

Trust in yourself. Trust in your knowing. Trust in your connection to the Divine. Trust in your guidance.

Trust is an issue that you may struggle with. Learning to trust self and others is important.

Allow yourself to develop trust in yourself, your intentions, and your connections to the divine will. Thrust in the magically unfolding of the divine plan in your life.

Judge Not

The lessons in your life and the lives of others cannot always be seen from the human perspective. Do not judge these experiences. Simply accept the lessons, and as you raise your vibrational frequency, you will no longer have need of many of them. Know that you, and they, may be choosing to experience something unpleasant so that you (and they) may help someone else later on. Trust that the people and events in your life are intentionally placed in your life path to facilitate your growth. Be open to all with a glad and appreciative heart. Judging causes a separation, instead move into unconditional acceptance.

Release Fear and Judgment

Learn to recognize fear and judgment as downward vibrational adjustments. Then simply choose not to have them. If you do feel the feelings associated with fear and judgment, allow them, and then learn to move beyond them. Fear lowers your frequency and judgment alters it. No longer are they needed and both serve no positive purpose for humanity at this time.

Fear and judgment keep humans from moving into their full power. Fear and judgment put Eartheans in a vibrational state which makes them open to control. Choose to release fear and judgment from your vibrational field.

When you feel fear's paralyzing effect on your energy system, do whatever you can do to get your energy moving again. Sing, dance, move or pray. All these will get your energy going, which dispels fear and its effects. Trust that what you do is right for you. You can always ask the angels for help; they do love to be of assistance.

If you catch yourself moving into judgment (especially against self), then choose to choose again. Release the judgment and move into loving acceptance of the person or situation—regardless of what it is. See it as a thought form moving into the light, where it is transformed into a thing of beauty. If moving from judgment to acceptance is your issue, you may pray/affirm the following:

I am divinely perfect. I accept who 1 am and what I am in this moment. I am open to change as I learn the lessons life offers me. I am aware that if I knew everything about everything and had reached a state of perfect perfection, I would have no need of the lessons Earth offers. I accept who I am fully and trust that I do my best in all situations. I am always open to growth and know that every day, in every way, I am getting better and better. I accept and honor myself and all that I am.

I recognize that all people on Earth are doing their personal best. They, too, are here for growth, and therefore I move from any judgment of others into total acceptance and honoring of their path. The Infinite Intelligence created diversity on Mother Earth, and I honor the wisdom of diversity in all things.

Honor and Respect All Paths and All Life Forms

All of the creation is holy and each is a part of the Oneness; therefore, to show dishonor to any aspect or member of creation is to dishonor the Creator. Native Americans consciously chose to walk in harmony with all creation. This is a respectful way to honor all creation. Everyone must willingly choose to do this. To walk in disharmony with all of creation is to choose to self-destruct.

We are moving into a 5D vibrational pattern that will not allow any form of disrespect to be shown to another. No longer will we be able to deny the personal power and influence of women, ethnic/racial groups, economic classes, and/or religious minorities No person will be able to increase his/her power by suppressing another's. All people will be honored regardless of age, weight, sexual orientation, or planet of origin. Plants, animals, and minerals will be honored for their role on this planet. All must be recognized and respected for their great contribution to life on Earth.

Thought has Power

Thoughts have power. They impact others and they impact the quality of your life. Think responsible. Thoughts are a basic form of creation and carry great influence on this planet. To think is to create.

To think of someone or something is to build an energy bridge to that person, place, or event. A bridge allows energy flow in both directions. If you open yourself, via your thoughts, to a lesser light, you allow that lesser energy into your existence. If you flood that being with light and love and then close the bridge, you have allowed your energy to impact theirs without allowing them to influence you. If you read, watch, and think about a tragedy, you allow that vibrational reality into your life. If you read, watch, and think about love, peace, harmony, the God Source, and so on, you also allow that vibrational reality into your life.

With each thought you have, you are both sending and receiving a vibrational energy that may or may not serve you. Each thought is a choice. You are responsible for all thoughts, whether they are intentional or not. Each thought must become an intentional act of creation.

One technique for truly becoming responsible is to speak aloud all your thoughts. This requires much courage and commitment, but it does make you fully aware and responsible for your thoughts.

Lighten up and Laugh at Life
Laughter holds a special power. It shifts your vibration and heals the heart.

Laugh at life. Life is a grand game designed by a loving and giving Creator/Source. Best not to take life too seriously. Life is meant to be fun. It is a game of your own design. Therefore, it is your responsibility to ask for all that is good and helpful for you and your world. Laugh at yourself for not asking for more.

Laughter helps to change your perspective of life. It loosens the self-forged chains in which humanity has wrapped itself. You serve humanity well when you can inspire laughter. Do not take life, yourself, or God's mission for you too seriously.

Keep Your Life in Balance. Be Open and Flexible

There is sometimes a tendency to run off to a mountain peak or a solitary cave to continue your spiritual growth. Your progress will have the most impact if you keep your life in balance. You need to learn to harmonize your physical, mental, and spiritual growth.

You have a physical body that eats, sleeps, feels emotions, cleans the floors and senses the 3D world around you. None of these are good or bad; they simply are. Experience them but do not become entrapped by them. Feel the pleasure and the comfort. Allow yourself to experience the abundance that life has to offer. Physical existence was never meant to be a life of hardship and lack. Pamper your body. Balance play with work, leisure with effort, and learn to appreciate each aspect for its unique contribution to your growth.

You have a mental mind that enjoys thinking, reasoning, learning, and growing. Use it. Turn your heavy-duty problems over to your mind before retiring to bed. Review the details and outline the problem. Let your mind work on the problem as you sleep. Upon arising, or when you least expect it, the solution will pop out of thin air. Thank your mind and show your appreciation, for this is the purpose for which it was intended.

Your ascension needs to be a part of a balanced life. You came to be part of this world; therefore, no matter how ascended you become, you are still expected to be a normal person. Enjoy your perfectly imperfect humanity. You may still need to keep your job, wash your dishes, take out the trash, and other such mundane tasks.

You may feel the need to read, meditate, sing, take classes, or pray all day. Remember "for all things there is a season." Keep your life in balance. Excess in any one area may slow your progress more than help it. You may feel the urge to go and preach to the world; this, too, may be counterproductive. Your loving, balanced life will be the model that most helps the world, and the world begins with your children, family, neighbors, and co-workers. Share your love, and the rest will take care of itself. You will serve your spiritual growth and your God Essence best by learning to love unconditionally. This, of course, comes from listening to your inner guidance. Learn to let go of anything and everything that is not in harmony with love.

Do not be surprised by a shifting of your priorities. Remain flexible and open. The important things of yesterday may not be the important things of tomorrow. Feel the shift from outer reality to inner reality. The goals you made for yourself last week may no longer be important today. Relax and go with the flow in the new direction.

Remember to Breathe
Breathe deep and slow. Watch a baby breathe and model your breathing after the child. Breathe from your belly; breathing activates more than your lungs. It opens you to receive the manna from heaven. When breathing properly, you pull in the ethers, which speeds clearing and opens both your mind and your cells. Set time to focus on your breathing and experience the rejuvenation in your body and soul.

Sleep peacefully
During sleep state, much spiritual work is done. It is also the time of reconnection to your higher self and spiritual guides. Most remember nothing about these meetings but this is the reason why so many problems seem so much easier to face after a good nights sleep.

It is also the reason why it can be difficult to sleep if you have a troubled consciousness, you know you must go and face the music and stand accountable for your actions. A prayer of release and forgiveness can often assist in falling to sleep.

Sleep is a necessary and important part of life, so enjoy it and keep it in balance. Too much or too little sleep can hurt as much as it can help. Your body, mind, and spirit need this time of rejuvenation.

Sleep time is a time when light volunteers can be hit with huge influxes of energy. It is one of the things you volunteered to do. The energy comes into your body and you, in turn, move it on, around, and into the Earth. Your physical body has the easiest time processing this energy when it is at rest. This energy infusion is usually accompanied by a release of body waste.

During sleep, you can also be called for active duty in other realms. You can sometimes spend more energy during these nightly excursions than you gain from sleep. Thus you wake up more tired than when you went to bed.

To give your body the sleep time it needs is easy. Sleep when you are tired and be active if you are not. Don't lie in bed complaining that you can't sleep, or force yourself to stay awake if you are tired. Consider sleep time a gift and use it accordingly. If you aren't tired keep going (I find I need less and less sleep) or if you are tired go to bed and surrender to your sleep. If I were to chart my sleep pattern, it would not be a consistent 7 hours a night. Rather it would be about 4-5 hours a night with spikes of 12 to 14 hours every month or so. As long as my body is strong and healthy, and I have plenty of energy during my awake time, then I know my body is getting its sleeping needs met.

Sleep is important for many reasons, physical and spiritual. It is important that this time of your life be seen as a sacred experience and very important to your spiritual growth. Make it a special time in your day.

Live Stress-Free

Stress is the result of how we see the experience. Since stress begins in the mind and is based on our attitude, what affects your attitude, controls your stress—either taking your stress level up or down at will. For instance, if I tell you that tomorrow you must give a three-minute presentation to your coworkers—this may induce great fear and trepidation in your mind, thus generating much stress in your life and body. (Fear of speaking is listed as the number one fear in US adults. Even greater than the fear of death.)

Your attitude toward the experience of giving the speech is causing your stress—it is not the speech but your reaction to the speech that is stressing you. Your body is having a physical and emotional response to the idea of the speech. If you liked giving the presentation, and you were anxious to share with your peers, then this would cause a very different response in your body and emotions. Whether you experience the positive or negative response is a product of your attitude.

The two main contributors to stress *that you control* are your beliefs (particularly about yourself) and your level of fear (especially fear of judgment) that affect your attitude which in turn determines your level of stress in any given situation. Think about the question that moves through a person's mind in a stressful situation: "What is going to happen?" (fear of the unknown); "Can I do this without looking like a fool?" or "What will they think of me?" (fear of judgment). Your level of confidence and your feelings of competence help determine your stress level.

As you experience life events or people that induce stress, recognize it and intentionally change your attitude and beliefs about the person, place, or thing. Then watch as your stress dissipates.

Stress is just one of the many ways that we are being kept from our greatness. Currently, on this planet, people are being systematically taught to be stressed. The media, in its many forms, are filling us with the belief that we are less than the greatness of who we are. The more people who accept this false belief they the more successful they are. If you reject it and continue on your path of truth, you and the Earth both win.

As you surrender to life's many experiences the stress subsides. As you become neutral or impersonal toward life, you experience no stress. As you know and trust you can handle anything that life gives you, you will live stress-free. Life will always provide opportunities for stress, but they are only offers of lessons to grow on. They can be viewed as roadblocks and setbacks, or as stepping stones and opportunities. It is your attitude toward them that will make all the difference.

Remember Your Source
Finally, as you drift off to sleep, remember who you really are—a child of the God Source, a spark of the pure God Essence. If you can remember the source of your greatness, you will more easily open to your divine inheritance. You are not a physical being trying to reconnect with your spiritual self. You are a spiritual being choosing to experience a physical reality. Regardless of your religious persuasions or lack thereof. You are very special. As Jesus reminded us, "Don't you know that ye are Gods." We are not **THE** God, but we are aspects of that divinity and as such we have unimaginable power available to us. As we claim our divinity and act in accordance with that divinity, we will allow more of our divine nature to be manifest in our daily life.

Begin today to see yourself as the light of the Radiant One. Visualize yourself as a being of light separate from your physical body. See yourself removing the crusty layers of restrictions, false beliefs and limiting behaviors that you have wrapped yourself in for so many years. Feel the vibrational shift as you hold this thought.

Awaken to all that you are and all that you can be. Awaken to your Divinity and mission. Mother Earth needs you. It is not about what you do, but who you are. Give yourself permission to be your greatness.

So be it.

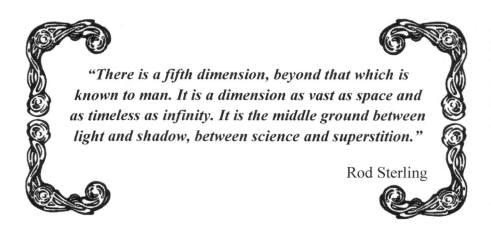

"There is a fifth dimension, beyond that which is known to man. It is a dimension as vast as space and as timeless as infinity. It is the middle ground between light and shadow, between science and superstition."

Rod Sterling

~16~

The Alpha and the Omega

"You are more than you can imagine and you live in a world much greater than you ever dared to dream."

Dr. Heather Harder

In the end, regardless of the actions and awareness of those who live on this planet, change will occur. The planetary shift from third to fifth dimension will occur. It is only a matter of when and how.

Until it is settled, your dimensional mind will shift. Often like a leaf in the wind. This is normal and to be expected. You are a reflection of what the Earth is going through and vice versa.

Beloved Mother Earth awaits patiently for the outcome.

Each thought, word, and deed chosen by every person living on earth determine how long and how severe the labor pains. Choose now to choose love, peace, unity, forgiveness, and compassion, and in that choice, Mother Earth is blessed. Focus your mind and heart on the things that make your soul sing and your vibration soars. This is the true mission of the Earth-based volunteers and the opportunity of each person in residence on this great planet.

If you are so moved, let the visualization serve you and the planet. It is powerful. This meditation was first given to me in 1993 and I have personally witnessed its power on many occasions.

I had been watching television when the weather man had announced that the weather patterns had frozen and was releasing a torrent of rain on the nearby Mississippi River. The old Mississippi was flooding its banks.

That statement caused me to shutter. I knew the weather patterns never freeze naturally—the very nature of nature is to be dynamic and ever changing. I immediately contacted my spirit friends and asked about it. I was reminded that the Earth-based volunteers are on this planet to transform themselves and this planet and that the struggle between the forces of light and the lesser lights (those who intentionally dim their light), had begun.

My spirit friends explained that the *one who will become known as the antichrist* was controlling the weather patterns. *I was told never to call him the antichrist as this empowers him but to refer to him as "the one who will become known as the antichrist." Not sure whether you want this capitalized or not. The next page it is not.*

This information came as a shock to me at many levels. I knew it was possible to manipulate many things with just our thoughts. In my own mind development process, I had been guided to use my thoughts to manipulate the clouds, dividing them, moving them around and dissolving them—always with permission. This helped me develop my mind powers in a healthy way.

I knew the process that was being used to control the weather, so I thought I might be able to help free them. I asked if there was anything which I could do to intervene with this manipulation of weather.

It was explained that if I interfered with this situation, I would be no better than him. This indeed was a drama that would play out on this planet and this was just the beginning. I was told that he was manipulating the weather because he knew that if he could make people hungry enough, by destroying the food crops, they would sell their soul for a loaf of bread.

I was told to just love him and to *send him love and light unconditionally. I was also told to send unconditional love and light to the Earth, to the weather patterns, to the atmosphere and to the mass consciousness of this planet.* This seemed doable although I was hoping for more.

I called two friends together and in the sacred space of my driveway, we said a prayer and sent out love to them as suggested. I called my friends, not because I couldn't do it alone, but because I know that two or more working in harmony for the same loving purpose are more powerful, and I wanted as much help as possible.

We spent probably about 2 minutes on this exercise—intention and faith are the precursors of success, not duration.

When the weather was next announced, the weather patterns had broken. Nature was back in motion. It may have all been coincidence, but I am not taking any chances.

Now, I regularly send love and I teach it to any and all who are interested. As you will see, I have expanded it and end it with giving the angelic forces this unconditional love and light to use for the good of this planet and its people.

For the record, when I tap into the energy of the one who will become known as the antichrist, I find a very smooth, charismatic energy. He is not evil or twisted as I would expect, rather his energy is charming and deceptive. He may even believe that he is working on behalf of the world's best interests, after all, he believes he knows the way to make everything better. All we must do is give him our power and he will take care of us.

Christ gave us a message to stand in our own power. He taught us to be responsible. He told us anything he did we could also do if we went within and discovered our own source of greatness. The opposite of this message is found in the person who will become known as the antichrist's message. "Give me your power and I will take care of you. Trust me and I will do it for you. Just go along and I will make everything better."

Not long after, in May 1993, many of the most famous psychics, channelers, and mystics were predicting that California was going to fall into the ocean. No problem for me, I live in Indiana I thought.

I was scheduled to travel to Bali to deliver some presentations and my journey took me through the LA airport during that very weekend. When I arrived at the LAX, I discovered my international flight had been postponed until the next day.

No surprise to me, I have given my permission to help the Earth in any way possible. Now I am in LA during a time most psychics thought it was going to fall into the ocean…hmmmm…I wondered what my role was to be. I knew I was to send love and let the universe send love through me into the earth.

While in LA, I could feel huge waves of energy flowing through me. Since I was trapped in an airport hotel, I productively spent my time in prayer and surrender to the process…as I am sure many other people were also doing.

Nothing ended up happening to California. Could it be that every psychic was wrong? Or perhaps had enough spiritual love work been done that the Earth was able to heal without amputating California? Certainly, I may never know for sure, but what I do know is that all the Earth-based volunteers have the power to make a difference, individually and collectively.

We Earth-based volunteers have taken on many issues in order to heal ourselves and thus heal the planet. In this healing process, many changes will occur, but the consequences of this personal healing are our primary objective.

Earth must heal in order to survive. Humanity's existence depends on it. We are living in the times referred to in many ancient prophecies. Collectively, we determine which ones or even how many of these prophecies will come to pass.

These times have often been called the "end times." And indeed they are, but this can be as simple and uneventful as the end of "clock-based time" as we know it. Time, as measured from an arbitrary perspective, will not be possible when we have moved into full power of thought manifestation. For our thoughts will affect it so greatly that it can no longer be considered a standard unit of measure. As Einstein discovered, "Time is relative."

But the "end times" can also refer to humanity's stubborn and stupid refusal to work out our differences between people and countries through peaceful, respectful and harmonious ways. In which case, we blow up the planet with our bigger and better bombs. Life of Earth ends as does the planet itself. Thus it really is the end times.

Collectively, we decide.

But we, the Earth-based volunteers. are here to make a difference. If we chose to use our light and our love, we can make a difference. Through our action or apathy, we decide the fate of this planet. Through our loving or judging thoughts, we determine the next step. Through accepting our differences or alienating those that are different, we choose. Through peace or war, we decide.

Every intention thought, word or action we take, we are moving closer to living an unlimited life of our potentiality or ending it all...and...we decide.

For every 1000 volunteers that come to this planet, only one will awaken to their divine mission. For every 1000 volunteers that awaken to their mission, only one will have the courage and conviction to live their mission (which is to fully awaken to their divine nature). This may sound discouraging, but for every volunteer that awakens to their divine nature, each has the power to negate the negative energy/impact of 10,000 people who don't! And when 2 or more gather for a common goal of good, those numbers, and positive influence becomes incomprehensible.

Never underestimate your power to make a difference, even with a single thought. The following guided visualization exercise is shared because I have found it very powerful and life altering. It was given to me by spirit and it has proved itself in many instances. Please use it often. Simply sit quietly and allow yourself to become a vessel of love. Pay attention to how you feel both before and after. Modify this visualization as you feel appropriate. Know the fate of the planet is in your heart.

Pay attention to your physical reaction as you experience this. Your body must integrate and assimilate these energies, and that isn't always easy. Change in diet, sleep, and elimination is just some of the issues you may experience.

Accelerating Earth's Energy: A Transformation Exercise

Open to your experience. Allow it to permeate your body. Feel the words and experience them in your imagination. Take three deep slow cleansing breaths to prepare for service to Mother Earth both spiritually and physically. With each breath, breathe in all energy vibrations. In your imagination, see yourself transmuting this energy to unconditional love. Exhale pure unconditional love energy. Each breath serves to support the loving personal and planetary transformation.

Imagine your most favorite spot on this planet. Lay down on the earth, belly to belly, and heart to heart. Stretch out your arms to embrace this living and loving Mother Earth.

Share your appreciation and gratitude for all that she does for you. Thank her for giving you this opportunity to experience life in physical body and for the range of lessons and emotions it brings.

Open your heart to her and the messages she sends.

Feel the love and appreciation being returned to you. Be open to receive the love and wisdom.

Earth is going through a great transition. You can assist in this personal and planetary transformation. Awaken to the light and love within your core. Empower this divine light and love. Imagine this ball of love grow and expand until it fills your world and all that that is within your awareness. Continue to expand this love and consciously combine it with the love and light of all those of like mind.

Send this love into the earth, filling every cell in, on and around her with this love.

Send this love out into the atmosphere, filling the atmosphere with this love. The atmosphere becomes a blanket of love keeping Earth safe and protected. The atmosphere is to the Earth as your skin is to your body.

Send love to the weather patterns. It is the Earth's weather that keeps the planet in balance. As I send love into the weather patterns, I help to bring peace, healing, and love to Earth and these locations of extreme weather.

Send love into the mass consciousness of the planet. The mass consciousness is the collective vibration of every thought, word, and action of all the Earth's residences from all times. The collective consciousness helps to determine the karmic and collective experiences of this planet. It determines the dimension individually and collectively. By sending love into the collective consciousness you help soften the Earth's collective experiences. Invite the angels to transmute all of your energetic contributions to their highest vibrations possible.

Send love to all leaders and candidates for leadership positions on this planet, elected, appointed or self-selected. By surrounding them with love, you give them the advantage of seeing truth clearly through love in order to help them make the wisest decisions possible at every level and in every situation.

Send love to all those who need or want love. Send love to all who are open to receive love. Give permission to the angels to use this love in any way that serves this planet or its people as you continue to bathe the Earth in love.

As you send love out to be used for divine purpose, also open your heart to receive even greater love in return. Universal law mandates all things sent, will be returned many-fold. Since you send only love, love can be returned to you.

In this state of love, willingly release all patterns, beliefs, behaviors that might limit or inhibit your ability to generate, absorb and use this love. Release anything and everything mechanical, emotional, intellectual, or ethereal that impedes this divine flow of love in your life. Surrender to your destiny. Allow all your wounds to be healed and your life to be a perfect expression of divine love made manifest.

So be it! It is so!

Claim your greatness which is your destiny. You are more than you ever imagined and you live in a world greater than you ever imaged.

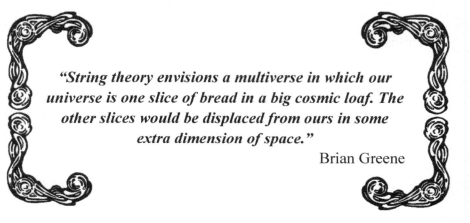

"String theory envisions a multiverse in which our universe is one slice of bread in a big cosmic loaf. The other slices would be displaced from ours in some extra dimension of space."

Brian Greene

Epilog: A Few Words from Heather

Dear Friend,

Thank you, dear reader, for taking time from your life to experience *__Dimensions & the Awakening of Divine Consciousness__*. Understanding the dimensions will empower you to confidently and compassionately take dominion over your world. Each step you take is a step toward knowing your true nature and experiencing the greatness of who you are.

You live in a world of your own making. You are not now, and never have been, a victim of it. You are the co-creator of your world and regardless of its condition, it serves your current needs and lessons. Of this I am positive.

I wish you great joy and happiness as you progress along your life's journey. There are multitudes of beings, both on this planet and beyond, who desire to assist you. Open your heart and mind to your greatest and most perfect Divine destiny and allow the God-of-your-knowing to guide and support you.

I present this book to you, not as an expert on the topic, but as a fellow traveler on the path of truth. It is my intention *__Dimensions & the Awakening of Divine Consciousness__* will challenge you as it has challenged me. I herald its release and celebrate its entry into the world. More importantly, I anxiously await its reception in your heart.

Send me your feedback. If you found *__Dimensions & the Awakening of Divine Consciousness__* helpful, tell me how. If you didn't, tell me why. Your empowerment is the reason I write (that and I am driven to share). What improvements has it made in your life? Write a testimonial and I will add it to my website or better yet, go to Amazon and add your comments. These reviews and testimonials are powerful and deeply appreciated. Is there a way I can improve this book? Are there questions I have left unanswered? Email me at heather@heatherharder.com now. I love and appreciate your feedback.

If you have benefited from this book, I hope you will do me the honor of sharing it with your friends and family. Having a group of friends that you can discuss and apply the information is vital to your continued growth. This isn't a book that you can read and forget, it must mingle with your thoughts and seep into your daily life. Many readers have found that joining a small book club is helpful. If you decide to do this let me know, I offer special discounts and can offer a book club kit.

Love and light for now and forever,

Heather Anne Harder, Ph.D.

Dr. Heather Anne Harder
heather@heatherharder.com
www.heatherharder.com

Additional Books & Products by
Dr. Heather Anne Harder

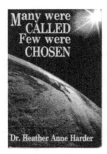

Many Were Called - Few Were Chosen: The Story of Mother Earth & the Earth-Based Volunteer

The awesome story of Mother Earth, from her perfect beginning to her threatened existence today, and of the Earth-based volunteers who've answered the call to aid her. If you are drawn to this book you're probably one of them.   ISBN# 1-884410-00-6 $13.95

Perfect Power in Consciousness

Learn the techniques to achieve balance and inner harmony by identifying and removing limiting behavior. This book outlines the physical, spiritual, and mental steps needed to achieve personal greatness. Learn to master the changes as you are led into a newer dimension of reality.

ISBN# 1-884410-01-4 $12.95

Exploring Life's Last Frontier: The World of Death, Dying and Letting Go

Life is a cycle. Death is a natural and healthy part of life. The book takes you beyond the living to experience the nature and process of death. As you become familiar with death and the experiences it brings, you will reduce the amount of fear and grief often associated with it. You will be guided through the ocean of terror that has surrounded the word "death" to a shore of peace and tranquility.   ISBN# 1-88134-30-3 $15.95

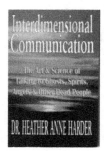

Interdimensional Communication: The Art & Science of Talking to Ghosts, Spirits, Angels & Other Dead People

Talking to people around the world is easy and there are a variety of ways to achieve it. Now talking to those outside the physical realm can be just as easy. Learn the process of interdimensional communication to reach a new & higher level of consciousness and connect with sources of all wisdom. Gain mastery of connecting with higher selves, angels, guides and others as you discover valuable insights into your life.   ISBN# 1-884410-14-6 $16.95

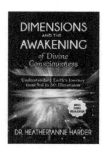

Dimensions & the Awakening of the Divine Consciousness: Understanding Earth's Journey from 3rd to 5th Dimension

The world is changing and so are we. Understanding these internal and external changes holds the key to a happy well-balanced personal and professional life. ___Dimensions & the Awakening of the Divine Consciousness___ shares humanity's journey from their third dimensional beginnings to the 4th dimensional a mindset to the ultimate state of fifth dimensional consciousness. This is the journey from a world of duality to a state of oneness. From a world defined by your five senses to a world defined by love and unity. This journey sounds simple. It is not. It requires courage as you are asked to reprogram your body and mind so that your true self, your soul essence, takes the lead in your life.
ISBN# 978-1543093612 $17.95

Go to **www.heatherharder.com** to see a full list of books, CDs, DVD and other resources available.

About Heather

Dr. Heather Anne Harder, Ph.D., was born a teacher, leader, and entrepreneur. When she was six years old, using her Dad's scrap lumber, she built her first school in the backyard. It wasn't big, but it had a roof, floor, and four walls and held six students. When completed, she recruited neighborhood children to fill her classroom. She knew, even as a young child if her classroom wasn't interesting, engaging, relevant, and fun, her students wouldn't come back. She mastered this lesson well. Her backyard classroom stayed full and the neighborhood mothers loved her. Over the years, her classroom has changed and her teaching venues have evolved, but she continues to provide the same kind of relevant, enriching, and engaging learning environment.

Today she is a nationally recognized thought leader and authority on human empowerment. As a professional speaker, author, consultant, and coach, Dr. Harder empowers organizations and goal-oriented individuals to shed their limitations and claim their super-self status. By combining a unique and exclusive blend of tools, techniques, spiritual strategies, magic and miracles, Dr. Harder challenges clients to step authentically into a bigger world, to dream bigger dreams, and live a life without self-imposed limitations spiritually, personally, and professionally. Her work changes lives, challenges people, and inspires organizations to reach beyond the ordinary and experience the extraordinary. Heather is an award-winning university professor and possesses the unique ability to tap into the Universal mind and then assess, articulate, and act as a catalyst for meaningful change. For over 25 years, she has worked with Fortune 500 companies, educational institutions, government agencies, healthcare organizations, and nonprofit endeavors. During this time she has challenged thousands of people to question and eliminate dated attitudes, assumptions, beliefs, and practices. She is a popular international speaker and author of books and hundreds of articles that challenge status quo and change lives through her inspired, occasionally controversial, and always thought-provoking insights. Her radical common sense interlaced with humor and profound truth, cause her audiences to willingly open their mind to new possibilities and potentialities. Heather has appeared on hundreds of radio and TV shows across the country and on such networks as CNN, CSPAN, MTV, NBC, and CBS. Check out her website: www.heatherharder.com and sign up for her Super Self Secrets Newsletter and to receive other notices and gifts.

She welcomes your comments, questions, and opposing beliefs. Send them to heather@heatherharder.com

Consult With Heather

How can I serve you? Do you need a quick boost to get over one of life's speed bumps? How about a speaker for your next event?

I love traveling the world sharing my wisdom, humor, and experiences with you. My mission is to awaken the world to fully understand exactly who they are and why they are here. Indeed, you are so much greater than you dare dream and the world is so much more complex than you can imagine. My greatest joy is to help you recognize and bring your best to everything you do professionally, personally, or spiritually. Everything is connected.

Here are a few ways you can continue to allow me to inspire you to live your greatness.

1. Go to my website www.heatherharder.com and subscribe to my newsletter and updates.
2. Review my books and read more of my writing.
3. Join me on a future trip or retreat.
4. Book me as a speaker. I have been an international professional speaker for more than 30 years. During this time, I have spoken to countless corporations, conferences, trade associations, churches, and organizations around the world. I am available for presentations including keynotes, seminar, webinar, and other live or virtual event.
5. Schedule me for a private consultation or hire me as a personal coach. Let me help you uncover what may be holding you back or what will catapult you forward in your life. If you feel you could benefit from one-on-one interactions with me, email me and tell me what you need.

For these or any other service email me at heather@heatherharder.com. I look forward to connecting with you.

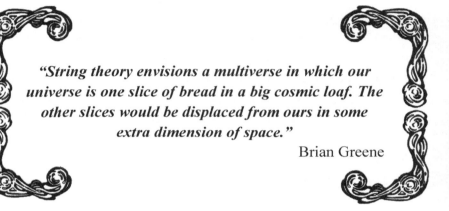

"*String theory envisions a multiverse in which our universe is one slice of bread in a big cosmic loaf. The other slices would be displaced from ours in some extra dimension of space.*"

Brian Greene

THE PERFECT SPEAKER FOR YOUR NEXT EVENT!

Any group, business, or professional organization that wants to empower their people to become greater and more successful than they dare imagine (regardless of how they measure success) needs to hire Dr. Heather Harder for their keynote and/or workshop training!

TO CONTACT OR BOOK HEATHER TO SPEAK:

Dr, Heather Harder

9800 Connecticut Drive

Crown Point, In 46307

219-662-7248

heather@heatherharder.com

Get Your FREE Gift Now

Thank you for your purchase of *__Dimensions & the Awakening of Divine Consciousness__*. You are another step closer to understanding your world and why you are here, now. As a planetary light volunteer (and if you are drawn to this book, you **are** a planetary light volunteer), your assignment is to shine your light on all you experience. The more you know, the better you are, and the brighter you shine. Being a lightworker isn't always easy but it is always appreciated.

There are some things that just can't be written. Explaining a Multidimensional Journey is one such thing. Therefore if you go to www.heatherharder.com/dimensionresources you will find several recordings of meditations, webinars, and video clips designed to further your understanding of the dimensional shift now taking place. The list of free resources grows with each new question and request.

My job, as as humanities alarm clock, is to wake you up and shake you up so you can accomplish your mission and achieve your Earthly purpose. I intend to nudge you into full consciousness and then into full action. What can I do to help you?

Indeed, you are more than you can imagine and you live in a world much greater than you ever dared to dream. It is my duty and honor to inform, empower, inspire, and encourage you to achieve your greatness. Whatever I can do to assist you on your journey, please ask. Send me your questions and comments.

It is important to learn about the spiritual practices but it is just as important to integrate them into your physical world. What good does being able to achieve interdimensional communication if you aren't able to achieve healthy communication with your spouse or children? Everything is connected. You must live in a balanced world.

I have created several tools and resources to help you on your journey. Go to www.heatherharder.com and sign up to receive my FREE newsletter and check out my other resources. I think you will enjoy them.

Made in the USA
Monee, IL
13 April 2023

31742798R00085